KU-492-573

THE CENTRE FOR ENVIRONMENTAL STUDIES SERIES
General Editor: David Donnison

THE FUTURE OF PLANNING

CENTRE FOR ENVIRONMENTAL STUDIES

Members of the Study Group on Developing Patterns of Urbanization

PETER COWAN,
Chairman of Study Group, Joint Unit for Planning Research, London

DAVID DONNISON,
Centre for Environmental Studies, London

CHRISTOPHER FOSTER,
London School of Economics and Political Science

PETER HALL,
University of Reading

EMRYS JONES,
London School of Economics and Political Science

BRIAN MCLOUGHLIN,
Centre for Environmental Studies, London

DEREK SENIOR,
Freelance Journalist

PETER WILLMOTT,
Institute of Community Studies, London

ALAN WILSON,
University of Leeds

DATE DUE FOR RETURN

The Future
of Planning

A Study Sponsored by the
Centre for Environmental Studies

Edited by
PETER COWAN

Director, Joint Unit for Planning Research,
London

 Heinemann · London

Heinemann Educational Books Ltd

London Edinburgh Melbourne
Toronto Auckland Johannesburg
Singapore Kuala Lumpur Hong Kong
Ibadan Nairobi New Delhi

ISBN 0 435 85920 X

© Joint Unit for Planning Research 1973

First published 1973

Published by Heinemann Educational Books Ltd
48 Charles Street, London W1X 8AH

Printed in Great Britain by
Richard Clay (The Chaucer Press), Ltd.,
Bungay, Suffolk

Contents

THE FUTURE OF PLANNING

Chapter One

Introduction

PETER COWAN

During the next thirty years people will become better off, better educated and more mobile physically and possibly socially. The suburbanization of rural areas outside the cities will continue apace, and more and more people will own their own house and garden. These trends will create problems. Social polarization may occur in our cities, with the rich moving into the suburbs, leaving the poor behind in the centres. Problems of poverty, colour and differential opportunity may grow in importance at the same time as living standards rise generally. Planners will need to think in terms of providing wider access to opportunities for a larger proportion of the population. As cities disperse at a regional scale they may reconcentrate at a local scale, creating new problems of accessibility and congestion in outer metropolitan areas. Unless national productivity increases much faster than it has in the past, or a much larger proportion of resources are devoted to construction, the rate of redeveloping the existing urban environment will not be rapid enough to enable past neglect to be made good or to support radical changes in the geographical pattern of urbanization. Above all the developing dialogue between the planners and the planned will be a major constraint, because any changes in the future pattern of urbanization ultimately require changes of mind, life styles and ways of thought which are quite profound. These are some of the conclusions which arose out of the first stage of our work on 'Developing Patterns of Urbanization', sponsored by the Centre for Environmental Studies, and published in 1970.

Such conclusions may not in themselves seem very startling. They are the sort of thing that any sensible person, taking a certain amount of thought and trouble, might spell out. But although by themselves the conclusions may seem trite, in combination they raise a formidable series of issues and problems to anyone concerned with the future of urban Britain.

The changes we described in the first stage of our work will have an enormous impact on planning. More people; bigger and more dispersed cities; a population at once better informed and more demanding; growing affluence and social and physical mobility—these and many other trends and patterns must affect profoundly what planners do and how they do it. What is more, the impact of technology upon planning is already being felt, and the application of new 'systems approaches' to the planning process is beginning to raise stresses and strains, inside and outside the town planning profession, which will reverberate through the next three decades. Thus the title of the present volume—'The Future of Planning'.

The General Perspective and Some Differences

A word is needed about our outlook and perspective. Most of us, as members of the working group, believe that planning is a necessary activity. If we suggest changes in the present array of activities and people involved in planning, it is not because we believe that (for example) the free market will necessarily solve problems better, but because we feel that planning can be improved. We recognize, of course, that the market is here to stay and that planning must work *with* market forces, but we believe that planning can be made to do this more effectively.

We do not adopt a passive 'trend-style' forecast. We have taken a positive view of what *ought* to happen. In the jargon of forecasting we are 'normative' rather than 'exploratory'. This position makes us at once more vulnerable and potentially more useful. Unless we provide some positive suggestions with which others can agree or disagree, it is difficult for the reader to respond to our work, either positively or negatively. We hope to stimulate more than this. The problems confronting planning are real and considerable, and it would be wrong simply to produce a critique without stating what we feel needs to be done.

Of course, while we have achieved a general consensus on the aims, scope and stance of planning and the issues which will face planners in the not too distant future, we have not been able to resolve all our differences. Thus there do remain some conflicts. For example David Donnison and Derek Senior differ in their views of neighbourhood councils and also about the prospects for provincial development and the resources and power base which this requires. Again there are differences between Christopher Foster's view of planning and the market, and the stance of some other chapters. We hope the reader will recognize their differences, for we have tried to make them explicit rather than smoothing things out into a bland façade. Planning has always generated debate and differences, and this book is no exception.

Problems of Definition

What do we mean by planning? We all try to plan our lives; and we are all subject to the attentions of various kinds of planning. Most of us, as private citizens, often feel more planned against than planning. How then shall we define the activity of public planning as opposed to what each of us does every day?

The dictionary is an obvious place to start. There seem to be two main definitions of 'planning'. The first is concerned with drawing or sketching plans, and is clearly not the kind of thing which forms the main focus of our work. The second part of the dictionary definition concerns 'making plans'; 'strategies' and so on—it is this which is of interest to us.

However, our focus is sharper than this. We are concerned with planning insofar as it affects patterns of urbanization. Yet even within the field of urban and regional studies, there are many different views about the meaning of 'planning'.

Some people suggest a very wide interpretation, according to which planning covers almost every aspect of human affairs in the modern western world. Others feel that a more limited definition should be adopted—tying planning closely to the physical environment. These varying interpretations often arise from individual views about the outlook of urban studies. Some people feel that it should be the task of research workers to help those working within the traditional fields of urban and regional planning, and that the main problems needing attention are those which concern spatial settlement patterns in Britain during the next few decades. Others suggest that one cannot hope to say anything about settlement patterns without discussing other non-spatial issues which may have a profound effect upon the kind of life which people are likely to choose in the next thirty years. They point to the United States, where physical and spatial rearrangements of cities have had little effect upon the central problems of urbanization, which appear to be educational, social and cultural in origin. Of course, it may be that the problems faced by cities in the United States are not as universal as some suppose, and that because of social and cultural differences Britain will experience quite different problems. But these unknown problems are just as likely to be based on social patterns, and a strictly physical interpretation may miss some of the most crucial issues for the future.

Our own focus has been on planning for the built environment, and we have adopted a fairly operational approach to individual issues as they have arisen. For example, we do not consider the spatial aspects of housing without giving due attention to the preferences of people for different styles of life, and to this extent our work has involved issues of social planning and goals. Similarly in transportation planning we need to consider not only technological and land-use aspects, but the social pattern of preferences and choices and the economic planning issues which surround them. It is plain that, in such cases, cultural and social issues can affect directly spatial issues, but there may be other areas in which the connection is more obscure.

We have therefore adopted a flexible interpretation which at some times is quite confined and at others extends into sociology, politics and economics. The main purpose of our book is to explore and discuss how planning is evolving, and what it may become. We define it by topic rather than in some abstract way. Even so the future of planning as we see it ranges much wider than traditional or professional views of 'town planning', beyond simple land-use considerations.

Of course, from the very nature of our subject we are concerned with growth and change. We are concerned with planning as a *process* rather than a static pattern-making activity.

But over and above this broad operational view of planning in general, we have described various *kinds* of planning. Thus we have 'spatial planning' and 'Comprehensive Strategic

Planning' (Peter Hall); 'Structural Planning', 'Policy Planning', and 'Corporate Planning' (Donnison and Senior), and
again 'Corporate Planning' (used in a different sense by Foster).
We have tried in each case to say exactly what we mean by
each of these terms, and although certain differences of interpretation do remain, we trust the reader will not be too confused
by a plethora of definitions.

Some General Points

Planning finds itself today more and more in the centre of the
political arena. Planning is an essentially political process
because it deals with the allocation of resources. Thus *ends* are
in question, and decisions are ultimately a matter of judgement.
These decisions are taken by an exercise of power. Moreover,
the decision-makers ask their advisors to clarify objectives and
formulate options and arguments for them, and to identify the
important issues. Planners have to be normative and it is part
of their professional task to do so, yet the fact that something
often happens as a result of the planner's actions calls for a high
degree of objectivity and a careful weighing of all factors without loss of commitment. We must distinguish between professional *objectivity* (meaning processes for getting things right and
introducing checks, validation procedures and so on) and
professional commitment. The opposite of objectivity is bias,
not neutrality; the opposite of commitment is neutrality, not
objectivity.

The sources of bias are many, but one lies in the data available to the planner and the way in which he uses it. There is
sometimes a temptation for the planner to take into account
what is easily measurable and to ignore or overlook other
factors in the planned environment. For this and other reasons
the integrity of planners is crucial to the future of planning.

This leads us on to the question of the use of new techniques
and their impact on planning. Many techniques which have
evolved outside the traditional field of 'town planning' will in
the years to come have an increasing effect upon the planner's
activities. Technological forecasting, systems analysis, model
building, and all the other techniques which form part of the
'new planning' are beginning to enable planners to anticipate
and act upon problems much earlier than in the past. At the

same time, these techniques are revealing the extremely complex nature of urban problems and the many interdependencies which exist in the urban scene. Such revealed complexity will have considerable consequences for planning. Ashby's law of Requisite Variety states that any complex system needs procedures of equivalent complexity to control it. Thus planning must evolve into a high variety system. Of course, it is possible to suggest that the market is an extremely high variety system, and that it is therefore the best mechanism for controlling and regulating urban and regional development. However, the degree to which the market should be free to operate raises another whole set of issues such as the extent to which certain groups of people will suffer, and over what time period, which lie somewhat outside the straightforward systems approach. These issues are examined at various points in this book, and while there are some conflicts over the degree to which intervention in the market should be encouraged, there is a general consensus that planning must take account of market processes and not be set entirely in opposition to them.

One issue which we have not dealt with explicitly but which is implicit in much of what we say concerns the ecological question and its relationship to urban growth and development. Planners have always been concerned with 'the quality of life', a theme which runs through the book. The latest metamorphosis of the ecological argument, that is to say that planners are trustees of the environment for future generations, is a resumption and restatement of a very old planning tradition. This theme recurs in our discussions of the new planning, the concern for public participation, the relationship between planning and government, and in many other places. Again, the growth of technological forecasting and other new techniques should help planners to anticipate ecological problems more effectively than in the past.

Some Themes and Threads

In addition to the theme of quality of life mentioned above, a number of other issues occur in the book. First, there is the issue of re-distribution, for we see planning as essentially concerned with the balance of opportunities between various sections of the population and areas of the country. Next, there is the issue mentioned above of the increasing complexity of planning and the problems this will pose both to the planner and the planned, who are increasingly demanding more access to the planning process. Again, as mentioned above, there is the question of the relationship between interventionism and the market. We see this as essentially a complementary relationship rather than a conflict. There is also the set of issues raised by participation, representation and government. Here we see major questions facing the planner in the definition and perception of issues and problems, and especially we see government itself as part of the plannable. Certainly we take a very open-ended view of government in both its central and peripheral power bases. These themes and threads are taken up in the concluding chapter.

The Question of International Perspective

There is another aspect to our work. How far should our views be confined to Britain and how far should they be more inter-national in range? Clearly there are many advantages in comparing the way planning might evolve and the problems it might encounter in other countries with the future of planning in Britain. First, other countries may have already faced and dealt with some of the problems which we have yet to en-counter. Second, planning is an international activity, and our work might be of more use to a wider range of people if we 'went international'.

People, goods and ideas cross international frontiers, and it is probably the third of these which is most relevant to our present purpose. Many of the most stimulating developments in planning during the past decade have come from abroad, especially from the United States, and have been taken up and modified as they reached this side of the Atlantic. The develop-ment of transportation studies, the use of Programme Planning and Budgeting Systems, the development of Advocacy Plan-ning, are obvious examples. In fact the volatile nature of planning in the United States seems to breed new ideas, techniques and approaches very rapidly indeed. Perhaps because of this, the recent history of planning in the United States follows a series of waves of enthusiasm, acceptance and rejection as each new idea is generated, tried out and abandoned. As these ideas are transferred to Britain, so the waves of enthusiasm and so on are damped down, so that ideas are modified, changed and incorporated into the ongoing development of the structure of British planning.

Of course the traffic in planning ideas is not all one way, and over the years many British planning ideas and inventions have been exported, and British planning skills are much in demand throughout the world. Thus it is important for us to bear in mind this international aspect to the future of planning, and we have tried to deal with it where necessary.

We suggest that there are two main reasons for dealing with a problem or issue at an international scale. First, when experience of another country helps us to describe what may happen here. Second, when events in other countries may directly *affect* what is likely to happen here. Thus our definition of international scope is, like our definition of planning, highly pragmatic.

We have tried to avoid taking these models from other countries as *fixes* for our own work. Where relevant we have used foreign examples, but we do not accept as a group the inevitability that planning style in Britain need follow any particular model. Thus, as we have said, the changing face of planning in the United States over the past decade has illustrated a number of problems, but many of these are different from those which will face British planning during the next thirty years, which is our primary concern.

The Shape of the Book

For such a complex problem the shape of our book is very simple indeed, and some may consider it too simple. We begin by discussing the issues which we think will face planning during the coming decades. This draws upon our previous work combined with other ideas which have been generated by our present activities. The next chapter sets out in broad terms how planning might respond to these issues. In combination with Chapter Two it acts as a 'hinge' between our previous work and the substance of the rest of the book. This is followed by two chapters, the first concerning planning education while the second is about the future of the planning profession. Clearly, if the tasks and techniques of planning are to change, so must the training and organization of planners. Next we have three Chapters describing the relationship of planning to three key sectors of society; government, the public, and the market. We suggest various problems which are likely to face planners and which they should begin to think about right away. Finally we bring together some of the main themes in the book and try to show the interrelationships between them.

This book has not been easy to write. We have aimed for a more coherent overall view than our previous book, which contained a series of relatively separate chapters, each written from an individual standpoint. Furthermore our subject and approach is more ideologically 'loaded' than our previous 'exploratory' forecasts. From a series of long and arduous debates we have achieved some kind of collective view of the future of planning. The various chapters are cross referenced and common arguments and ideas carry through most of the book. We hope the reader will find our efforts of some interest, and although it would be foolish to expect everyone to agree with all our views, we hope at least to stimulate further thought on this most crucial topic.

Chapter Two

The Tasks for Planning

PETER WILLMOTT

The previous volume was about some of the likely changes in Britain up to the turn of the century; one chapter in particular discussed some trends in society—in family and community life, in social class and in people's aspirations.[1] As explained in Chapter One, the present book is about how planning is likely to—and, to some extent, ought to—develop in response to those changes. The purpose of this chapter is to act as something of a bridge between the two. Drawing upon the earlier papers, it tries to summarize the main questions that are likely to form the tasks for the planners of the 1980s and 1990s.

There is a prior question. In order to form a view about how 'planning' should respond to a changing society, we need to know what 'planning' is. If we conceive of it in the narrowest 'town-and-country planning' sense, the issues with which it will need to be concerned will be mainly spatial. If we conceive of it more broadly, the issues will be correspondingly broader. Our starting point—and in a sense the theme of this book as a whole—is that the conception of 'planning' held both among professional planners and in British society more generally has widened and is likely to go on widening, and that partly in consequence the issues that will, over the next three decades, be thought of as problems for 'planning' and 'planners' will be non-spatial as well as spatial.

The scope of planning has broadened for a variety of reasons,

---

[1] P. Willmott, 'Some Social Trends' in *Developing Patterns of Urbanization* (Edinburgh: Oliver and Boyd, 1970, pp. 8–30).

some of which are discussed more fully in later chapters. For one thing, the last decade has seen rapid developments in the techniques of planning, particularly the growing use of mathematical models to simulate how cities and regions work and, in local government more generally, the increasing emphasis on methods of programming and budgetary control. There has at the same time been a growing concern about the social consequences of spatial policies. There are a number of different strands in this change:

1. *Interdependencies.* It has become increasingly clear that almost every act by central or local government in any specified geographical area both influences and is influenced by almost everything else that government does. Thus at the regional level transport planning, industrial and employment policy, recreation planning, planning for higher education, housing policies, social security and taxation policies and many more all bear upon each other and upon land-use planning. An illustration at a more local level has been given by David Donnison:

> The economic and social influences working upon us tend to have a mutually reinforcing character. In future the planners must ensure that vicious spirals grow virtuous. We should ask not merely whether the slums are being cleared or whether schoolchildren grow healthier—separate questions about different aspects of life, directed to different public services. We should be asking whether the location and distribution of housing ensure that the most deprived children attend schools where there are good teachers, and sufficient numbers of able and ambitious children to make high attainment a feasible and respectable aspiration; and whether the opportunities for work and leisure open to pupils from these schools are of a kind to encourage high attainment; and whether public transport and the location of housing and industry gives everyone access to these opportunities; and whether family allowances, rate rebates, housing subsidies and other systems of income redistribution work in ways that extend the aspirations of the deprived, rather than restricting them; . . . and much else besides.[1]

2. *Unintended consequences of policy.* The quotation from Donnison touches on a particular aspect of the general point.

---

[1] D. V. Donnison, 'Liberty, Equality and Fraternity', *The Three Banks Review*, December 1970.

There has been growing anxiety, voiced among others by R. E. Pahl,[1] that recent policies have had unexpected, and pre-sumably unintended, social results, in particular in making some sections of the urban population worse off relative to others.

3. *Relationship to the economic market-place.* Planners used to think of themselves as something like policemen, regulating economic traffic that was originated elsewhere by others. They are coming to recognize that they themselves generate some of the economic traffic and that they can help others in the market to make their own plans, whether to buy a particular house for owner-occupation or to invest £100 million in new industry, in convenient and mutually reconcilable ways. In other words, planning is seen not as the antithesis or alternative to the market but as something that itself influences and mediates market operations. There is a growing realization that, in consequence, planners need to understand market mechanisms more fully and use them more wisely than they have in the past.

4. *The concern with 'environment'.* The last decade has seen the growth of campaigns against 'environmental pollution' and for the preservation and improvement of the 'environment'. A cynic might point out that the slogans are often invoked simply to justify the protection of particular local interests. But the concern about the environmental consequences of public policies—and of the activities of private industries—is certainly proper. The wide questions posed about the future of the envir-onment, about problems of ecology and about population growth *are* crucial; they are not discussed in any detail in this book only because they have been very fully aired elsewhere.[2] But, again, the concern with such issues implies that one has to look more broadly than in the past at 'planning' and its consequences.

---

[1] R. E. Pahl, *Whose City?* (Harlow: Longman, 1970).
[2] See, for example, J. L. Fisher and N. Potter, *World Prospects for Natural Resources: Some Projections of Demand and Indications of Supply to the Year 2000* (Baltimore: Johns Hopkins, Plan for Resources to the Future Inc., 1964) and *The Population Crisis and the Use of World Resources* (World Academy of Art and Science, American Division, 1969).

5. *Participation*. There has, in the last decade, been a pro-liferation of local preservation and amenity societies, and of campaigns against what are thought to be the deleterious 'social' as well as 'environmental' consequences of planning proposals. The demand for 'participation' is thus another ex-pression of the platitude that at bottom 'planning is for people'.[1]

These various threads overlap and reinforce each other. They add up to a view of planning which is more wide-ranging in its interests, more sensitive to the multitude of cross-influences, and above all informed by more fundamental social values. The sights have been raised. It is now increasingly accepted that ultimate judgements about policies must be made in terms not just of tidy land-use or of the success of transport proposals or relocation policies, but of the consequences of these and much more for people's 'quality of life'. That is the yardstick by which planning and public policy in general will be judged.

Affluence and its Consequences

The confident prediction of increasing affluence in our earlier book—it was suggested that average real income per head would be double or treble the current level by A.D. 2000[2]—has been somewhat shaken in recent years. It now seems less probable that economic growth will be at such a high rate, and likely that Kahn and Weiner will prove right in their forecast that the United Kingdom would drop into the second rank of industrial nations, overtaken by countries like Italy and Spain.[3] Never-theless we are virtually certain in the long run to go on getting richer, as a nation and as individual consumers. Over the past century, the Gross National Product has increased at something like two per cent each year on average, and during the next thirty years neither short-term economic setbacks nor the increasingly lively intellectual debate about the validity of

---

[1] *People and Planning*, Report of the (Skeffington) Committee on Partici-pation in Planning, (London: H.M.S.O., 1969).
[2] M. Abrams, 'Consumption in the Year 2000' in M. Young (ed.), *Forecasting and the Social Sciences* (London: Heinemann, 1968, p. 37) was quoted, with endorsement, in 'Some Social Trends', *op. cit.* p. 11.
[3] H. Kahn and A. Weiner, *The Year 2000* (London, Macmillan, 1967).

economic growth as a collective goal seem likely to check that general trend. Despite the criticism of growth as an objective in its own right, anxiety about the 'quality of life' will surely be expressed more as a concern over the ways in which the fruits of growth are used than as an argument that there should not be any. The planning machinery will therefore continue to operate in a society geared to increasing (if only slowly increasing) affluence.

The trends of past decades, and a contemporary comparison of the spending habits and life-styles of richer people with those of poorer, leave little doubt about the main spatial implications. The number of separate households will continue to grow, with more young, single people in particular setting up in independent homes of their own. More families will buy more spacious homes in suburban or exurban areas; they will also buy the cars that both create the more dispersed residential pattern and are demanded by it. On present trends, by 1990 something like eighty per cent of British households will at least one car. Mainly because of the continuing ascendance of the private motor car, other activities—employment, shopping, leisure—will go on dispersing as well. The 'city' will continue to spread. The model for the future will increasingly be the urban region—a geographically dispersed 'city' (if it can still be called that) in which the old emphasis on movement along a few heavily-used radial public transport lines from suburb to centre gives way to a 'network' pattern of transport, based on the private car and criss-crossing every segment of the region.

Such a geographical pattern, plus high levels of car owner-ship, higher real incomes and more 'middle-class' styles of life, involves more physical movement. The general trend to a home-centred life will probably continue, though more people will also follow the present-day middle class in travelling longer distances when outside their home. The gradual increase in leisure time, mainly in the form of longer annual holidays, and (possibly) longer weekends, will encourage the same tendency. So will a steady increase in 'second homes'. Higher real incomes will increase the demand for leisure activities that need more space and more travelling—golf, horse-riding, climbing, country walking, caravanning, and above all sailing and other water sports of all kinds.

These predicted trends in life and leisure, together with the continuing geographical dispersal that they imply, will increase the demand for space around the present conurbations. The pressure will be intensified by the expected increase in population. The current official estimate is that the population of the United Kingdom will increase to 66 million by 2001 [1] but, because so little is known about the dynamics of family growth, this figure could prove several million out,[2] and additional growth of a few million would put greater demands on space, particularly in the regions already most heavily populated.

All this raises a question about national policy for the distribution of population, employment and investment between the different regions. The problem is familiar. Some regions, notably the South-East and the West Midlands, have faster rates of economic growth than others and are therefore attracting more investment. The concern about this is partly because, with increasing pressure on land, these 'popular' regions may become unpleasantly crowded. It is also, more importantly, because of the needs of the 'declining' regions. As a result of the industrial changes of the last century, these have large populations, albeit ones increasingly 'unbalanced' towards the older age-groups, but they are failing to attract enough new 'growth' industry. How is government to decide on the right balance between what could from one point of view be described as 'investing to bring new life to the regions', and from another as 'spending public money in trying to persuade private industry to go to regions where, on economic grounds, it does not want to go'?

During the next thirty years, this question of regional balance will move on to an international level as well. Britain will increasingly find itself involved in European-wide decisions about investment. The choice will be, indeed already is, not between the Tilbury container port and the nineteenth century London docks, but between Tilbury and Rotterdam's Europort. Or, to give another example, the discussion about airport location—with all its economic and other planning implications

---

[1] J. Thompson, 'The Growth of Population to the End of the Century' *Social Trends* No. 1, (London: H.M.S.O., 1970, p. 22).
[2] *Ibid.*, p. 23.

—will in the future have to take into account not just Speke and Prestwick but the airport strategy of northern Europe as a whole.

Dispersal, Concentration and Transport

Inside Britain the general trend is towards further dispersal within regions. But this raises a series of important questions, partly about what, in more detail, is likely, and partly about what is desirable and might be deliberately planned for. The two aspects—the pressures and the possible control over them—are inextricably mingled.

One question is about the degree of dispersal from the cities. Clearly, some further dispersal is inevitable. But how much? After, say, thirty years, what, on present trends, is likely to be the balance, in population and area, between the existing built-up areas and the new areas of settlement? What *ought* to be the balance? And what would be the consequences, to take opposite extremes, of a free market in development or of a deliberate planning strategy to renew older urban areas and strengthen their attraction?

There is also a question about the balance within the outer areas themselves. Given further dispersal from inner built-up area to outer ring, what will be and what should be the extent of concentration or dispersal within the outer ring itself? Is population to be dispersed within such rings, or concentrated? Are shopping, employment and other activities to be concentrated, and at what scale? Are the areas of concentration to be mainly in existing centres, or in new ones? As Peter Hall has put it:

> As city regions disperse on the regional scale, are they to re-concentrate on a local scale? How far should localized high density nodes of activity, linked to high density public transport but with inevitable congestion limiting private transport, be permitted and even encouraged in the growing outer peripheries of our great metropolitan regions?[1]

---

[1] P. Hall, 'Transportation' in *Developing Patterns of Urbanization, op. cit.* p. 156.

It seems as if individual consumer choice is likely to encourage dispersal rather than re-concentration; despite current planning, that is probably the direction in which we are heading. But there are a number of powerful social and planning arguments in favour of concentration. One is the problem of the substantial minority of people who need public transport because they are members of households which, even in a society with high and growing car ownership per household, do not have a car at all.

As was noted earlier, about 80 per cent of British households are likely to have a car by 1990, but that means that 20 per cent will still not have one and, if American experience is any guide, this 'residual' proportion is unlikely to fall much in the following decades. Between 1954 and 1963, though the proportion of households in the United States with two or more cars increased from 9 per cent to 16 per cent, the proportion with no car fell hardly at all—from 27 per cent to 23 per cent.[1] The members of these—mainly poor—households clearly suffer from the deficiencies of public transport in spread-out cities like Los Angeles, and this has been partly blamed for the Watts black riots in 1965:

> Our investigation has brought into clear focus the fact that the inadequate and costly transportation currently existing throughout the Los Angeles area seriously restricts the residents of the disadvantaged areas such as south central Los Angeles. This lack of adequate transportation handicaps them in seeking and holding jobs, attending schools, shopping and fulfilling other needs.[2]

Quite apart from those households that are too poor to afford a car, public transport is obviously also important to some members of the households that do have one. If there is one car and the husband uses it for work, for example, the wife and other family members are dependent on public transport. Until every adult had his own car—and every child can have

---

[1] Walter H. Bottiny, 'Trends in Automobile Ownership and Indicators of Saturation' *Highway Research Record*, No. 106, 1966, pp. 1–21.
[2] California Governor's Commission on the Los Angeles riots, *Violence in the City—an End or a Beginning?* 1965, p. 65. Quoted in John F. Kain and John R. Meyer, 'Transportation and Poverty', *The Public Interest*, Number 18, 1970, pp. 75–87.

another member of the family as chauffeur—public transport will continue to be a major issue, as part of the general planning concern with accessibility and with the influence of settlement patterns upon it.

Transport also poses a series of questions at the local level. There will be more travel, as we have suggested, and particularly by private car. It is already obvious that this generates almost insatiable demands—demands for garaging or parking in residential areas, demands for parking in central districts and other shopping areas, demands for roads between and within urban areas. These demands come into conflict with others. Every local survey and many local campaigns bring up the same urban issues about which people are exercised—not enough parking in central areas, too many parked cars destroying the environment in residential areas; too many cars in total but more families who 'need' them; the noise and danger of traffic but the frustrations of congestion; houses threatened by new road plans but still not enough roads. Such conflicts are bound to spread and intensify in the coming decades. They are conflicts not just between different sorts of people but often between the same people in different rôles—as residents, as motorists, as ratepayers, as urbanites. The planning issues may arise in many forms. Should a shopping area be closed to traffic? Should motorists pay, through one of the new schemes now under discussion, for the road space they use? How far should one-way and other traffic management schemes be introduced? What is the right balance between the need for urban motorways and the need for amenity or conservation? These are all variations on the issue posed by Buchanan: how can an urban society be reconciled to the car, and how much are its citizens prepared to pay for such a reconciliation?

The Consequences for Cities

The main trend in the pattern of settlement—that towards greater geographical dispersal—obviously affects not only the suburban and rural areas which are gaining population, but also the older urban areas that are losing it. As long as the people moved out but jobs and other functions stayed inside London and the other cities, the result was an increase in commuting. But when, as now seems to be happening, the central areas begin to lose industry and other functions, the threat to the inner cities becomes serious indeed. It is made still more so by the fact that the inner areas of most of Britain's cities were built about a hundred years ago, so that much of their housing is due for renewal or rehabilitation.

Changes in the regional balance of social classes are one indication of the dangers. What seems to be happening is that there is more social class segregation between each conurbation centre and the surrounding parts of its region. In some cities, notably London, there are fashionable inner areas which continue to attract well-off people, but the general trend is for poorer people to stay inside the cities and for better-off people to move outside.[1]

A special comparison of the occupational distribution in different zones of the London Region between 1951 and 1966 has shown that over the fifteen years there was in the Region as a whole an occupational 'up-grading', as there was in the country generally. But the balance was certainly changing. The proportions in the Registrar-General's top two 'social classes' increased by 3 per cent in Inner London, 5 per cent in Outer Greater London and 7 per cent in the Outer Metropolitan Area; the proportions in the bottom two classes fell by 3 per cent, 3 per cent and 6 per cent respectively.[2] There has similarly been a growing demographic segregation, with the old and the young more often living inside cities and the growing families outside. Census comparisons show, for instance, that the proportion of people aged 15 to 24 increased by 4 per cent in Inner London, 2 per cent in Outer Greater London and 1 per cent in the Outer Metropolitan Area between 1951 and 1966.

As the sets of figures show, these processes have not yet gone very far, though the trends seem clear enough. But a central question is whether such changes in balance matter anyway. The Greater London Council certainly think they do; they fear

---

[1] D. E. C. Eversley, 'Old Cities, Falling Populations and Rising Costs', *Quarterly Research Bulletin*, Greater London Council, June 1972; *Strategic Plan for the South East, Studies* Volume 2, *Social and Environmental Aspects*, H.M.S.O., 1971.
[2] P. Willmott and M. Young, 'Social Class and Geography' in D. E. C. Eversley and D. V. Donnison (ed.), *Planning of London: Some Aspects of Socio-Economic Change*, forthcoming.

something like the decline of city centres that has already occurred in the United States.[1] The Town and Country Planning Association, among others, take the opposite view; they argue that all that is important is a reasonable balance of occupational, age and other divisions inside a region as a whole, and that 'specialization' within it is both inevitable and perfectly acceptable.[2] The judgement naturally influences the policies proposed. On one view, the planning task is to arrest the processes that are in train. On the other, it is to accept and even encourage them, and to tackle in a different way the problems of those who remain in inner city areas. It is obvious that the two different diagnoses lead not only to different planning policies but also to different conclusions about the government of regions (or, more likely, the different views about *that* lead to the different diagnoses).

The above discussion of balance has been within regions, but a similar question arises at a more local level. On this, even the facts are in dispute. Again the example is London, because more statistics have been collected about trends within it than for other cities. Some evidence seems to suggest an increasing concentration of poor people (or poor and very rich people) inside particular local areas or zones of Greater London; other evidence points the other way.[3] Opinions differ about which evidence is most convincing. Whatever the facts, there is disagreement too about whether 'social balance' inside local areas (implying some spread of different social classes in their local population) is either a feasible or desirable objective of policy.

Again, different conclusions follow about what should be done. On one view, many inner city areas are becoming more 'unbalanced' in social class or age or both, and one way to ease the problems of such areas is to encourage the movement in of different kinds of people so as to strengthen the local economic base and improve local shopping, services and amenities. On the other view, either there has been no change or, if there has, the main way to deal with it is by further extensions of the Plowden policy of 'positive discrimination'—allocating a larger

---

[1] See e.g. Greater London Council *G.L.D.P. Inquiry Proof* EIII/I, p. 30.

[2] T.C.P.A., *London Under Stress*, 1970.

[3] M. Harris, 'Social Polarization' in D. E. C. Eversley and D. V. Donnison, *op. cit.*

share of public resources to the schools and services in relatively 'deprived' areas. Of course this policy—or for that matter the alternative one—could also be advocated by people who did not think that there has been any change in 'social mix' but who recognized that certain inner city areas contained relatively large proportions of poor people and thus had special problems.

The preceding discussion illustrates the mixture of spatial and non-spatial elements, and underlines the fact that policies to deal with urban 'planning' problems involve much more than land-use and transport planning. Of course there are clear spatial or 'environmental' problems. One example is what is happening to housing and the physical environment generally in most of the older inner urban areas. The Milner Holland report showed, again for London, that while housing standards had risen in general, they had been falling in particular areas of dereliction—while most people had better housing, more space and more amenities than before, some had worse.[1] The task of renewal and rehabilitation in these derelict areas is formidable. At present many of them are deteriorating faster than they are being redeveloped. The process is likely to continue, as Peter Stone has pointed out:

> Unless national productivity increases much faster than it has in the past, or a much larger proportion of resources are devoted to construction, the rate of redeveloping the existing urban environment will not be sufficiently rapid to enable . . . past neglect to be made and standards substantially raised. . . .[2]

Enough has been said to show that the problem of the declining areas is not simply one of finding—or willing—the resources for rebuilding or renewal. The problems are also—and more fundamentally—to do with the distribution of opportunity. In all British cities there are older inner areas where housing is poor and opportunities limited. There are areas in which mainly poor people live (and perhaps, as already suggested, an increasing concentration of poor people). Though not all people with

---

[1] *Report of the Committee on Housing in Greater London*, Cmnd. 2605, H.M.S.O., 1965.
[2] P. A. Stone, 'Resources and the Economic Framework' in *Developing Patterns of Urbanization, op. cit.* p. 333.

black and brown skins are poor, the same geographical areas are the ones in which they too are concentrated. The residents of such areas suffer not only because they have low incomes, as many have, and therefore low living standards. They also have limited opportunities in the housing market, both private and public. Most of them cannot afford private transport and so their mobility is limited, their journey to work may be awkward and uncomfortable and in consequence their employment opportunities constrained.[1] Thus such areas present major tasks for planning in the coming decades.

The problems will need to be tackled at a variety of levels. Certainly the right regional and national policies will be needed. In the local community, one approach is that discussed by David Donnison in Chapter 6—a concerted attack upon the full range of deprivations of such 'urban priority areas'.

Affluence and the Distribution of Opportunities

The issues raised in this chapter fall under three main headings. One is the general point raised at the beginning: planning will increasingly be regarded as covering a broad spectrum of interests, non-spatial as well as spatial, and will be judged by its effects upon people's 'quality of life'. The second set of issues, more specifically, is to do with the consequences of affluence—more consumer goods, more suburban-style housing, more leisure, the spread of middle-class values and the geographical spread of the city that this seems almost automatically to imply. The worries are mainly about what happens to people who move out of cities and to the areas where they go. The third set of issues is located much more inside the cities; the worries are about particular areas, their physical environment and the opportunities of the poorer residents living in them.

The contradiction between these last two sets of problems— those that flow from affluence and those that concern the urban poor—is more apparent than real. Societies, as they become richer, do not automatically become more egalitarian. It is

[1] See R. E. Pahl, *op. cit.* and *Strategic Plan for the South East, Studies* Volume 2, *op. cit.* (see footnote 1 on p. 19).

true, as David Donnison[1] and Anthony Crosland[2] have recently argued, that an expanding economy offers a better base for income redistribution and of increased spending on public services, and European comparisons suggest that in recent years public spending has been greater in those countries with higher growth rates.[3] But redistribution is not automatic. J. E. Meade has, indeed, suggested that the emphasis on growth actually encourages wider differences of wealth, unless deliberate measures are taken to counteract this.[4]

It seems from this that, despite growing affluence, despite the spread of middle-class standards and styles of life over broad sections of British society, questions about the distribution of welfare will probably become more important in the decades ahead. There are obvious implications for planning, as crucial as the problems of urban dispersal and transport. Looking ahead over the next thirty years, it seems likely that planning will be dominated by the broad themes outlined in this chapter —the concern with the quality of people's lives, the need to come to terms with the environmental consequences of economic growth and the fundamental questions about the distribution of opportunities.

---

[1] D. V. Donnison, *op. cit.*

[2] A. Crosland, *A Social Democratic Britain*, Fabian Society, 1970.

[3] D. V. Donnison, *op. cit.*

[4] J. E. Meade, *Efficiency, Equality and the Ownership of Property*, Allen and Unwin, 1964.

Chapter Three

How Planning can Respond to New Issues

ALAN WILSON

1. Introduction

It is commonly acknowledged (throughout this book and much more widely) that the issues of concern to planners have changed and have expanded in scope in recent years. There is, of course, a continuing concern with the physical infrastructure and spatial organization of the city or region, but there is a growing recognition that other plannable factors also influence the people's 'quality of life'.[1] It remains usual and useful, however, to discuss many issues in planning in terms of physical infrastructure and spatial organization, noting that the important task is to evaluate the impact of any changes on 'quality of life'.

Thus, in the previous chapter, in an assumed context of economic and population growth, the main issues are concerned with dispersal, the rôle of central areas, 'balance' in outer areas, and the supporting transport system. It is emphasized in that chapter that it is particularly important to trace impacts on disadvantaged groups, and especially the poor. By definition, poor people have low incomes, and hence inadequate command over resources related to housing, and various services. It is quickly clear in this kind of discussion that everything depends on everything else, which complicates the

---

[1] P. Willmott, preceding chapter.

problems for the planner enormously. If the planner tackles any one stated issue, then the responses to his actions often have a variety of impacts unconnected with the original issue. This is the essential problem to be tackled in this chapter: given new issues, given their complexity and mutual interdependence, how can the planner respond? The problem is tackled by the introduction of a set of concepts which can be used to show explicitly the full complexity of the planner's problems (and which discourages short cuts in the search for solutions). They begin to form the basis for solving some of the problems. We begin by offering brief definitions of these concepts.

2. Some Definitions

We begin by accepting the 'systems approach' to planning.[1] We do this for two reasons: firstly, because the systems concept emphasizes notions of interdependence between sub-systems (or components); secondly, there is a tradition of systems analysis which involves bringing all relevant knowledge to bear on the system of interest, and hence provides a first-principles basis for our study, rather than a disciplinary basis. Thus, we refer to the city (or city-region or set of cities) as an urban system. We shall assume that it is made up of a social system, a resource system and a planning system. These sub-systems are more or less distinct, but overlap in the sense that people play rôles in each.[2]

The social system consists of the individuals and households of the urban system (referred to briefly as 'households' for convenience). The resource system consists of almost everything else: natural resources in the usual sense, houses, buildings and other physical infrastructure, but perhaps most important of all, the organizations of the city which create

---

[1] J. B. McLoughlin, *Urban and regional planning: a systems approach*, Faber and Faber, London, 1969; G. Chadwick, *A systems view of planning*, Pergamon, Oxford, 1971.

[2] Note that these systems are defined simply in terms of their components; no connotation of 'equilibrium' of related concepts is implied—as in Parson's systems, for example, discussed in Chapter 10 of W. Isard *et al.*, *General theory, social, political, economic and regional*, M.I.T. Press, Cambridge, Mass., 1969.

B

goods and services, partly for households and partly for each other, and which create new resources. (As a special case, the spatial organization of the city can also be considered a resource —partly produced by the planning system.) The information available in the organizations of the resource system is perhaps the most important resource—and this statement emphasizes the breadth of our definition of the concept of 'resource'.[1] The planning system is a particular set of organizations (considered for our purposes as abstracted from the resource system as a special interest in this analysis) which attempts to partially control the city for the 'public good'.[2]

We define the 'public good' to be 'net benefits' in the social system. Hence, the goals which planners are trying to achieve on behalf of households will be referred to as *social goals*. Planners will also formulate objectives in relation to the resource system, and these will be referred to as *resource objectives*. We define planners' instruments of control to be *public policy instruments*. We now have a conceptually simple picture of the operation of a planning system: the planners set their public policy instruments within the urban system to attempt to achieve stated resource objectives and stated social goals. These concepts will provide us with a basis for the study of the complex planning issues outlined earlier and discussed in the previous chapter. It should be emphasized that the object of developing this simple picture is to be able to represent the new issues which planners face. Perhaps paradoxically, the complex nature of these issues is revealed by the picture. It is possible, however, to develop alternative frameworks, and the reader is, of course, free to do so. The test of effectiveness of any such framework will then relate to its ability to display the structure of the new issues.

We discuss in turn social goals, resource objectives and public policy instruments (sections 3–5), and, later, their inter-relationship within a planning process (section 8). As a preliminary to section 8, we discuss the problems of measuring social goal-achievement (section 6) and the nature of the planning

---

[1] In this we follow Meier, for example, in R. L. Meier, *A communications theory for urban growth*, M.I.T. Press, Cambridge, Mass., 1964.

[2] The social and resource systems together will be referred to as the 'city', although strictly, of course, the planning system is part of the city also.

system as a control system (section 7). In the final section, we draw together a number of conclusions and implications of this analysis for the future of planning, and relate these to the discussions in subsequent chapters of this book.

3. Social Goals

We begin by considering the notion of household utility. There are many ways in which the variables of a utility function can be described, but initially we consider five broad headings:[1] shelter, subsistence and general well-being, breadth of activity opportunities, environment and income (job). A variety of particular household wants or needs could be listed under each of these broad headings. They are, as usual with this kind of list, interrelated. The notion of 'shelter' is easily understood and it is straightforward to develop, at least intuitively, a concept of progressively 'better' housing representing increasing utility through the progression. 'Subsistence and general well-being' relates to the consumption of goods and services primarily—food, health and welfare services, and so on. At any particular point in time, the members of a household will take a number of decisions which result in them spending their available time and resources in various ways, and a utility can be associated with these decisions. This alone, however, is not an entirely satisfactory measure of utility, as we feel intuitively that the range of choice from which the decisions were made itself reflects the level of utility achieved. It is intended that this should be measured through the third heading, 'breadth of activity opportunities'. This also includes opportunities to meet people, opportunities for development and access to 'better' jobs, and so on. As a special case, this may include learning and educational opportunities; education may also be considered a

---

[1] For a more detailed discussion, see, for example, A. G. Wilson, 'Some recent developments in micro-economic approaches to modelling household behaviour, with special reference to spatio-temporal organization', Paper II, *Papers in Urban and Regional Analysis* (London: Pion); it is possible to consider these kinds of broad headings as higher order branches of one of Strotz's utility trees, with income as the usual final variable—see R. Strotz, 'The empirical implications of a utility tree', *Econometrica*, **25**, pp. 269–80, 1957.

'job' if it is full time. We can assume that the quality of life is enhanced through a 'good' environment, though we should be careful to distinguish the variety of scales at which this comment applies—house and its immediate environment, locality, city, region and so on. We can also include notions of safety, security and acceptable political system (which would involve goals associated with both efficiency and democracy in government), and so on, with the concept of environment in this broad heading.[1] For those members of households who are employed, much of their time is spent in their employment, and so we expect our utility measure to be associated with their job in this way; further, and perhaps even more important, most household income is derived from employment, and this determines in large part the command over all resources of that household, so it seems important to list 'income' explicitly among our basic headings. In this context, we must also be concerned with the distribution of income. (This notion is illustrated in more detail in the previous chapter where Peter Willmott discusses the difficulties of people with low incomes.)

We have now defined some headings under which we can discuss social goals. Note that the headings do not refer to goals directly, but to what might be called areas-of-concern within which we try to formulate explicit goals. This can be a useful concept, especially as it may be feasible to construct goal-achievement indicators in relation to areas-of-concern, and then to formulate goals explicitly in terms of improvements in these indicators. It is also implicit in the discussions so far that areas-of-concern are associated with the activities of members of households.

Of course, even within an income group, households will have widely differing goals. Further, conflicts will often arise because some households will try to achieve goals which will prevent other households from achieving theirs. Thus, in all

---

[1] Note that this is one way of solving the aggregation problem: all the other headings except the 'environment' one refer to the private life of the household—the environment 'heading' records that household's perception of what everyone else is doing. The other 'aggregate' heading, which is implicit, relates to the transport system, the effect of which appears in terms of access to goods and services, activity opportunities and jobs.

our work we must try to establish measurements of goals-achievement which can be taken when these are aggregated. We should also explicitly recognize the conflicts which will exist in the system.

The activities of members of households utilize resources, and, in an obvious way, goal-achievement (that is the movement from one pattern of activities to another preferred set of activities for households) is through the consumption of resources. We can consider formally that the resource system makes resources available for these purposes.

It is hoped that the issues with which we are concerned in relation to the notion of 'quality of life' can be explicitly studied in this kind of framework. For example, in relation to the discussion of the position of poor people in cities, we assume that they have aspirations to achieve higher incomes, and hence more command over resources, an improved environment, greater range of opportunities from which to select their activities, higher level of goods and services, and higher quality housing. In each of these areas of concern, it is possible, at least in principle (though with some difficulty as will be discussed below), to construct goal-achievement indicators. It would then be possible to formulate goals in terms of minimum incomes, quality of environment not worse than such and such, and so on. The principal conflict arises through shortage of resources. Everyone will agree that the kind of goals sketched above for poor people are good in principle, but typically society is only prepared to finance (that is supply the resources for) relatively small improvements in goal-achievement indicators. This illustrates the complexity of the associated problem for planners: in particular, whose goals are to be the planners' goals—the goals of the poor people themselves, or the goals for poor people which the rest of society is prepared to recommend? We shall assume that such conflicts are discussed and partially resolved in the political system to which the planner connects, and that some planning goals—which might change from time to time with changing circumstances or changing balance of power—represent the resulting compromise.

In general, then, it is usually easy to identify the correct directions of improvement in relation to particular areas of concern, and hence to formulate specific goals (though not always; consider housing densities in relation to privacy,

environmental standards, sociability and development opportunities through meeting other people), but the planning issues
arise essentially either out of resource constraints or conflicts
about goals.

4. Resource Objectives

The sort of resources in relation to which planners might have
objectives are organizations (essentially the economic subsystem: manufacturing industry, private services, public services and so on), housing (public and private), the transport
system, the land use system and spatial organization of the
city and the physical environment. It is interesting to note that
plans are usually stated in terms of what we shall call resource
objectives rather than in terms of social goals. This can be seen,
for example, in relation to the headings in the new Development Plan Manual.[1] Then, because of the complexity of the
inter-relationship between resource objectives and social goals,
this could lead to inefficiencies.

Resource objectives may be of the following kind: to plan
for economic growth at x per cent per annum; to plan the interrelationship of growth in different economic sectors to maintain
a safe ecological balance and a high quality physical environment; to achieve a supply of housing with a certain distribution
of sizes and qualities; to provide an uncongested transport
system; to provide a degree of spatial organization in the city,
specified in terms of land-use, which ensures a proper interrelationship of different facilities. Clearly, even at this level it
is impossible to specify resource objectives without at least an
implicit reference to resource utilization, and hence to social
goals.

This concept of resource objectives is close to the notion of
inputs in a PPB (Planning, Programming, Budgeting) System,
while measurements of social goal achievement is close to the
notions of outputs in such a framework. However, this analogy
will not be pressed too far, as it is then possible to avoid some
of the rigidities which have developed in overformalized PPB
systems.

---

[1] Ministry of Housing and Local Government and Welsh Office, *Development plans: a manual on form and content*, H.M.S.O., London, 1970.

5. Public Policy Instruments

There seem to be four main types of public policy instrument: public expenditure (capital and current); public regulation; fiscal and monetary policies; form of governmental organization.

The proportion of expenditure in a national or local urban economy which is public may vary considerably, and the fixing of this proportion is in itself a policy instrument. When the planners' budget has been determined, he can spend it in a large variety of ways—on the physical infrastructure of the city, on public services, and so on. The relevant aspects of public regulation include land-use control, traffic management and company law. A wide range of fiscal and monetary policies, ranging for example from petrol tax to selective employment tax, obviously have an influence on urban development. Finally, the form of governmental organization itself has a major impact in both functional and spatial dimensions. Some authorities with a functional basis at present have considerable autonomy—Water Boards, Hospital Boards and Public Transport Authorities, for example—others, such as Education and the planning function itself are part of a governmental structure with more general responsibilities, and behaviour can differ accordingly. In various ways, central, regional (Economic Planning Councils, Standing Conferences of Planning Authorities, and so on) and city governments have an impact on urban development, and the form of development may depend on the relative balance of power and allocation of responsibilities. The inter-relationship of the different tiers of government are complex. The spatial organization of urban government is currently being restructured, of course, following the recent Royal Commission.[1]

The public policy instruments, then, are exercised by a large number of agencies, and within a legal framework which is being continually modified. What we have called the planning system is a part of this wider governmental system, and it may be called the planning technology and the governmental

---

[1] Royal Commission on Local Government in England, *Report*, Cmnd. 4040, H.M.S.O., London, 1969.

technology of the time. This notion carries with it the implication that we can invent new planning and governmental technologies to meet new situations, and this is, of course, one of our main concerns throughout this book. The related questions are discussed in more depth in Chapter Six.

6. Social Goal-Achievement Indicators

One of the biggest problems within the framework presented is the measurement of goal-achievement and the corresponding problem of developing criteria for the evaluation of alternative plans.

The simplest procedure is to try to develop indicators of goal achievement. It would be possible to work through the list of social goals (initially as areas-of-concern, but broken down in more detail than in the earlier presentation) and to formulate indicators such that a change in indicator value corresponds to a change for better or for worse in that aspect of the social system. This is often a useful thing to do. It is also useful to attempt to achieve progressively more detail. For example, the most discussed housing indicators at present are 'total built last year', 'total shortage' and so on, and there is a need to break this down by type in relation to different deeds at different locations. This immediately starts to beg many questions of value, both in relation to particular social goals, and relatively among the goals. These questions are nearly always particularly difficult, for the obvious reason that all good foreseeable projects cannot be carried out because of resource constraints or inter-group conflicts. So, except in very simple cases, indicators are likely to be unsatisfactory as evaluation criteria. However, such exercises will usually be worthwhile in the absence of anything better.

The next step is to see how we might do better. The obvious way of doing this is to look to welfare economics, which begins to offer a theoretical framework for discussing questions of value. All the methods developed so far turn out to be less than satisfactory for a number of reasons. For example, it is very difficult to ascertain and measure preferences and utility functions empirically (though we should go on trying); also, welfare economics only distinguishes Pareto optimality—A is better than B, someone is better off under A while no one is worse off

—this is rather weak. It does not distinguish adequately between distributional effects in many states which produce the same aggregate utility, though some progress has been made in recent years with the development of social welfare functions which do make such distinctions.[1] Other recent research work is beginning usefully to extend traditional welfare economics to examine social and planning questions as well as economic ones[2]—for example, work on the value of time, and the formulation of utility functions in terms of activities (rather than consumption of goods and services),[3] taking account of time budgets and environmental and inter-activity constraints as well as money budgets. But all this has a long way to go.

The tone of this section is perhaps too pessimistic. A good range of indicators can be developed in relation to each area of concern, and perhaps the level of progress in welfare economics has been underestimated—although the remaining empirical questions are very great. Nonetheless, a great deal of useful information can be produced, and at the very least the information base of political decisions should be dramatically improved.[4]

---

[1] See, for example, C. D. Foster, 'Social welfare functions in cost-benefit analysis', in J. Lawrence (ed.), *Operations research and the social sciences*, Tavistock, 1965.

[2] A. G. Wilson and R. Kirwan, 'Measuring the benefits of urban transportation improvements', *Working Paper 43*, Centre for Environmental Studies, London, 1969; A. W. Evans, *The valuation of time*, mimeo, Department of Economic and Social Research, University of Glasgow, 1969; A. G. Wilson, 'Some development in micro-economic approaches . . .' *op. cit.*; W. Isard *et al.*, *General theory. . . .*, *op. cit.* Chapter 12.

[3] K. J. Lancaster, 'A new approach to consumer theory', *Journal of Political Economy*, **74**, pp. 132–57, 1965.

[4] There are routes to developing indicators other than via the concepts of welfare economics, for example. For a social survey method, see P. Willmott and M. Young, 'How urgent are London's motorways?', *New Society*, no. 428, pp. 1036–7, 10 December 1970; for something in between social survey and welfare, economics, see G. Hoinville, 'Evaluating Community Preferences', *Environment and Planning*, **3**, pp. 35–50, 1971; for a straightforward indicator approach to one well-defined problem (racial segregation in the housing market) see B. J. L. Berry, 'Monitoring trends, forecasting change and evaluating goal achievement in the urban environment', in M. Chisholm, A. Frey and P. Haggett (eds.) *Regional Forecasting*, Butterworth, London, 1971.

7. The Planning System as a Control System: Requisite Variety

We earlier introduced the notion of the planning system as a control system. So far, we have only used the notion of a system for definitional convenience; now, we can utilize a theorem from systems theory. Firstly, we must define the variety of the system. Formally, this can be defined as the number of possible states which the system could conceivably get into; informally, it is roughly the degree of complexity in the system. The fundamental law of system control—the law of requisite variety, due to Ashby[1]—states that to be effective, the control system must have at least the variety of the system it is attempting to control.

It is easy to see that the city is a system of very high variety, while most planning systems are of relatively low variety. However, the way this statement is viewed depends on system definition. The planning system exercises controls in order that the people in the social system achieve social goals. However many social goals are achieved privately through market processes, and a little thought reveals a market as a high variety control system. There is an obvious implication that market processes may be of particular importance in relation to social goal-achievement as a complement to the public planning system. The relationship between the planning and the market is discussed in Chapter Eight below. It is also interesting to note that the increasing demand for public participation in planning can be viewed as an attempt to increase the variety in the public planning system, and in its extreme form this would create something like a market. This is discussed in Chapter Seven.

All this is not to argue that markets will solve the most serious planning problems—far from it, for all the well-known reasons related to the market imperfections. The essential point being made here is that it should be possible to investigate what the planning system is trying to control using available governmental technology, and then to check whether the control system has requisite variety. In the case of a deficiency in variety, it is worth noting that the solution is almost always to

---

[1] W. Ross Ashby, *An Introduction to cybernetics*, Chapman and Hall, London, 1956.

try to increase the variety of the control system (for example, by building in variety generators of the type discussed by Beer) [1] and not to reduce variety in the system being controlled, (which is what dictators do by repressive regulation).

The notions introduced above should encourage us to review certain existing planning 'policies' in this context. For example, it is often a stated policy not to mix land-uses in particular zones of cities. This may be a device used by the planners to reduce system variety, and hence appear to make their problems more tractable. It may be that this restriction could be usefully dropped, provided that there was a corresponding increase in variety in the planning system.

Relatively few studies have been carried out to try to estimate what planning actually achieves—that is, the degree of control which it achieves. We now see that such a study would be particularly interesting.

8. Goals, Objectives and Instruments: Inter-relationships Within a Planning Process

In terms of the concepts developed in this chapter, a plan is a setting of the public policy instruments together with a statement of the resource objectives and the social goals which the planners believe will be achieved by these settings. We can note a number of inter-relationships among our concepts. Firstly, the operation of a single policy instrument will often contribute to several resource objectives. For example, expenditure on a road will contribute directly to the resource objective concerned with the transport system, but may also contribute to a housing objective by facilitating a private development of housing in a particular place, and to an economic objective because it accelerates growth, improving efficiency in the economy by facilitating inter-organizational linkages. Secondly, the achievement of a resource objective will often contribute to several social goals. For example, public expenditure on housing may contribute directly to housing objectives, but also to the economic objectives by adding to a local labour force in an area where there is a labour shortage, and to accessibility

---

[1] S. Beer, *Decision and control*, John Wiley, London, 1967.

goals and transport objectives by relocating people from a more-congested area to a less-congested one. Further, housing development contributes obviously to goals concerned with shelter and related utilities, but also to those concerned with health and possibly education (because its location may be more assessible to 'better' educational facilities).

If we put each policy instrument in a box, each resource objective in a box, and each social goal in a box, then the relationships just described are like those shown in Figure 1. The immense complexities of modern planning arise in part because of the existence of the networks shown in this figure. We have indicated through some of the examples mentioned above that (given that we can measure goal-achievement) we can in principle trace the impact of a particular setting for a particular policy instrument—that is we can trace trees in the network from bottom to top. The great complexities of problems in urban planning arise because in practice we often have to proceed from top to bottom; given social goals, how do we achieve settings of public policy instruments to achieve these? Again, the existence of the network shown in the figure, coupled with the difficulties of prediction, make this a very difficult question to answer. (The theory of control systems may indicate for us the theoretical limits of what can be achieved.) And, of course, real planning problems are much more difficult than we have implied by the figure, which uses broad headings only. In practice, much more detail is needed.

The difficulty of discovering and tracing downward routes through the network of Figure 1 is essentially the difficulty of design in the planning process,[1] while the difficulty of prediction and tracing the impact of settings of public policy instruments —that is tracing upward routes in the figure—is the difficulty of analysis.[2] In this way, we can relate the concepts introduced

---

[1] This is one way of seeing that the design problem in planning is a major combinatorial problem; of course, the designer must seek 'organizing concepts' (C. Alexander, *Notes on the synthesis of form*, Harvard University Press, Cambridge, Mass., 1960), or 'guiding principles' (W. Isard *et al.*, *General theory. . . ., op. cit.*).

[2] A forward-looking review of modelling problems in this kind of analysis is given in A. G. Wilson, 'On some problems in urban and regional modelling', in M. Chisholm, A. Frey and P. Haggett (eds.) *Regional Forecasting*, Butterworth, London, 1971.

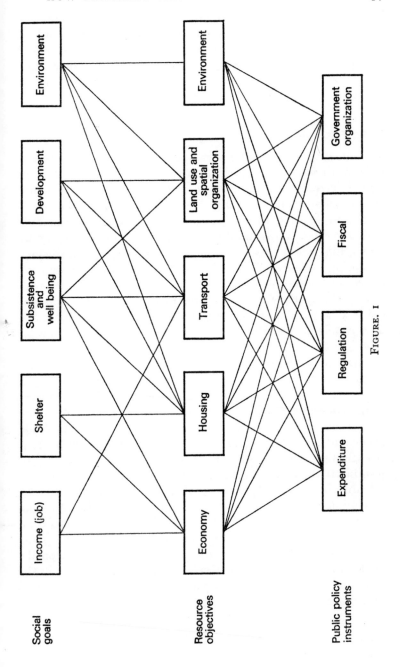

FIGURE. I

in this chapter to the conceptualization of the planning process presented in the equivalent chapter of our earlier book[1] in which planning activities were characterized as being concerned with policy, design (in the broad sense of generating alternative plans) and analysis. This whole chapter, of course, is an elaboration of the notion of 'policy' in that context.

9. An Example

To illustrate some of the ideas presented in rather abstract fashion above, we can consider an example. Suppose that, in some city centre residential area, a community living in 'slum' accommodation is identified. We would say that this represented an unacceptable standard of shelter, and hence that we had identified a planning problem. In traditional planning terms, this would be seen as an essentially physical problem— a housing problem. That is, it would be seen as what we have called a resource problem.

In terms of the framework presented above, we would first see it as a social problem, an area-of-concern. It is identified as a problem of shelter, but our framework demands that for any 'solution' to this problem, we trace the impact of this solution on other social goals, or areas of concern. We may discover in the course of such investigations that the problem of shelter is not even the primary problem for some members of the community—the main problem may be associated with accessibility (measured in terms of physical access or 'skill' access) to employment and an associated income deficiency. An effective *comprehensive* solution to the problem may only be possible if the issue is tackled, and this in turn may only be solvable in terms of provision of access to opportunities for education and training. Even if this kind of analysis does not apply to some members of the slum community, such problems may be generated by a purely 'housing' solution. Further, any solution for the slum community may have an impact on the goal-achievement indicator levels of other communities in the city, and these secondary impacts must be traced, measured and evaluated.

[1] A. G. Wilson, 'Forecasting planning', pp. 69–89 in P. Cowan (ed.) *Developing patterns of urbanization*, Oliver and Boyd, Edinburgh, 1970.

The resource objective with which we are most obviously concerned relates to housing. Housing in any of three tenure groups (private rented, public rented and owner-occupied) may be relevant. For example, by providing or encouraging the provision of some kind of private housing to meet the needs of a non-slum community, a filtering process may be generated which provides older, but adequate, housing for some of the people in renewal areas. This may be more suitable, for example by being cheaper, than providing new public rental housing. Other resource objectives—for example relating to public services and transport facilities, may be relevant directly to the slum community, and indirectly by modifying the filtering behaviour of other groups. Thus the resource objectives, as we would expect, may be set in a variety of ways, and, again, a comprehensive approach is needed.

It will be now equally clear that a great variety of settings of the public policy instruments could generate any one set of resource objectives. These are the obvious possibilities of spending available public money on housing, through to less obvious forms of expenditure on roads and services which would indirectly generate a housing supply, by encouraging private development and possibly a filtering process, for the slum community.

We can summarize by saying that there are likely to be many possible end-states which are of equal value in goal-achievement terms, and there are many ways in which each one of these end-states can be achieved. Many new issues are generated for the planner by the breadth of the view which has been produced by this framework. He must try to trace and measure all impacts, and attempt to find solutions which are efficient in a comprehensive sense. Efficiency in this context relates to both efficient use of resources and, within resource-constraints and conflict-constraints, providing people with what they want.

10. The Planning Skills Needed

A vast range of skills must be employed in a planning process if it is to be effective. Many social scientists, economists, sociologists, geographers, social psychologists and political scientists, for example, have an interest in at least some aspects of cities, and the skills available at the highest levels of these disciplines are needed to facilitate the analysis tasks—to measure goal-achievement (and the obverse of this, problem analysis), and to trace impacts of settings of policy instruments. Some of these people will study mainly the social system, others the inter-relationship of social system and resource system—the latter partly the creation of architects and engineers. Within such a planning process, the familiar deployment of professional skills will have to be developed further if an improving analytical capability is to be fully utilized. The role and possible roles of government in the system, especially in relation to the problem of public-government contact and the nature of public representation, will be very important. This in itself generates the need for skills in public administration and politics. In the end, only outstanding leadership and enlightened political decision-making will lead to the full utilization of the analytical and professional skills which could be provided.

And yet an amalgam of 'old' disciplinary skills will not be good enough; out of the old disciplines will develop a breed of people to whom the city is their primary system of interest. Between them (for it may be beyond the scope of one man or one 'new' discipline), they will begin to understand the interdependencies in the urban system, employing concepts and theories which are partly new and partly eclectically culled from other disciplines, and will deploy this knowledge within the planning process. The town planner attempts to do this now, along with his practice of design skills, but inevitably he is a jack-of-all-trades. Some of these issues are discussed in Chapters Four and Five.

The whole situation is complicated by the accelerating rate of change of the issues and the fact that the (as yet inadequate) new techniques—which might arise in any of the disciplines mentioned above—developed in response to these issues, often utilize concepts which are out of reach (without further training) of most existing practitioners. The fact that most of the disciplines and most developing techniques use a wide range of mathematical concepts is an obvious example.

We thus see two possibly conflicting demands: for more specialist skills of the highest order within the planning process, and for more systems analytical skills, which may be called, in one sense, generalist: hence the recently stated need for generalized specialists.[1] A corollary of this situation is that planning will find that it has an increasing internal communication problem. This will be partly solved by the systems analysts, partly by old-style generalists such as civil service administrators, and possibly, almost paradoxically, by the development of yet another new specialist skill.

Inevitably, this kind of discussion is rather abstract. In reality, the 'planning process', as it affects a particular area, will be made up of a multitude of interacting organizations—probably necessarily so in order to achieve requisite variety. It is an ongoing task to relate our abstract concepts to the jobs of such organizations. It is hoped, however, that the outcomes of this task will cast a new light on the planners' jobs.

11. Planning's Response to New Issues

It is not difficult, in a brief mental exercise, to compare the issues outlined in the previous chapter and in this chapter with those with which planners are mostly concerned today. We find what is fashionably called a large credibility gap. The previous chapter demonstrated the need for concern with the planners' statements of issues and evaluation of related peoples' quality of life above all, and with ways of relating to policies in these terms. The present chapter has developed a similar theme by employing the concept of social goals, and formally relating these to resource objectives and public policy instruments.

We have seen that an example of an important issue (and probably of a worsening one) is the plight of poor people in cities. Each chapter, in different ways, has demonstrated the complexity of the planning problem associated with this issue. Perhaps, in a sense, there is one and only one simple solution: to increase the income of poor people. It may be argued that no amount of planning of spatial organization, public housing or transport systems will be effective unless accompanied by a significant redistribution of real income. It is this sort of situation which has led Banfield to suggest that most *feasible*

---

[1] Lady Sharp, *Transport planning: the men for the job*, H.M.S.O., for Ministry of Transport, London, 1970.

solutions to the most serious urban problems are not *acceptable*.[1] Certainly present planning responses to these kinds of problem do not encourage optimism.[2]

Nonetheless, we hope we have shown that new procedures can be developed *in principle*, even though the associated analytical problems are very difficult, and the associated governmental problems perhaps even more so.

The framework presented in this chapter encourages us to be more explicit and wide-ranging in our consideration of social goals and alternative futures. The framework also forces us to take account of a high level of interdependence explicitly. The focus on the problems of measurement of social goal-achievement forces us to concentrate on the most serious planning problems instead of shifting our attention to more easily solvable ones. Our study of the nature of control systems forces us to be increasingly realistic about what can be achieved with a given planning system (instruments and policies), though it opens up again (following the introduction of the concept previously[3] an area of *meta-planning*—developing adequate policies in government about the planning and governmental system itself. In other words, one of the most important issues of concern to planners is the invention of adequate governmental technology.

What does all this mean for the future of planning in the next thirty years? As is usual in this kind of essay, we have outlined far more problems than solutions, but perhaps two broad conclusions can be drawn. Firstly we conjecture that, given high, and probably increasingly higher, rates of both technological and social change, there may always be more problems than solutions. When problems are 'solved', more difficult problems (either new problems or newly perceived problems) will be just around the corner. The planning system

---

[1] E. C. Banfield, *The unheavenly city*, Little, Brown, Boston, 1968.

[2] See, for example, the Birmingham Evening Mail, 23 February 1970, reporting the case of a family of nine whose rent jumped from £1.35 to £6.20 out of an income of less than £20 per week. The wife is quoted as saying: '. . . we soon found everything beyond our means. The only answer is to go back to the city, even to a slum, because I could keep it clean and tidy. At least, we would be able to afford to live'.

[3] A. G. Wilson, 'Forecasting planning', *op. cit.*

may have to budget for an increasingly large proportion of its own share of available resources to be devoted to research. It follows that the planning system must be a highly adaptive, responsive, high-variety system containing the highest level analytical and design skills. Using the terminology of Schon,[1] the centrally oriented rather authoritarian model of the planning system we have known until recently will be replaced by a diffuse (and actually much stronger) 'pools of competence' model. This will enable a much wider range of skills to be potentially available to tackle new problems as they occur. The development of manpower for such a system creates tremendous educational problems, which are discussed in Chapter Four. The planners in this system cease to look like the members of a single profession, and this creates another range of problems which are discussed in Chapter Five.

The second major conclusion arises from the concern with quality of life (or social goals). This raises a number of obvious value questions, which lead to the conclusion that the planning system must be more *connected* to the people. In other words, it must be much more outward-looking. Some of the problems of planning and the public are tackled in Chapter Seven. Other questions relate to planning and government (Chapter Six) and to planning and markets (Chapter Eight).

---

[1] Donald A. Schon, *Beyond the stable state*, Temple Smith, London, 1971.

Chapter Four

Manpower and Education

PETER HALL

The central question of this chapter is: what sort of education shall we need up to the year 2000 to train people who will call themselves professional planners? A subsidiary question is: what scale of education will be needed? The two questions are closely connected, for both depend on the answer to a more basic question: what shall we mean by planning during that period?

The time-scale is important. For the future, we may well have to accept a much more rapid cycle of technical obsolescence and retraining than in the past—a point that will be discussed in more detail later. Nevertheless we cannot doubt that decisions taken now will affect immediately the education of planners who, however defined, will still be practising—and, indeed, occupying some of the critical top decision-making jobs —in the early twenty-first century. The question 'what sort of planning?' demands the ability to predict.

Some Definitions of Planning

An approximation to the answer has been given in the immediately preceding chapters. It is that the definition of the word 'planning' has changed quite radically in recent years. Up to about 1960, and for many practitioners even later, planning was a term reserved for an activity concerned with the spatial arrangement of activities and the land uses that accommodated them on the earth's surface. The central uses which accommodated those activities were co-ordinated by a public authority which had the power to allow or refuse changes proposed by private individuals or groups. The intentions of the public authority were set out in a plan, which was a physical document illustrating present spatial patterns and the changes in those patterns which the authority would either make itself, or permit others to make, over a period of time. Subsequently, until the revision of the plan, the public authority would make its own investments, and regulate the investments of others, in accordance with it.

The system worked on the basis that land-use planning was an activity in its own right, with well-understood and generally accepted objectives, about which there was no need for extended public debate. The objectives were set out, in so far as they were set out at all, in physical terms: they included containment of large urban areas, protection of the countryside and the creation of self-contained and balanced communities. Only occasionally, as in the Barlow report of 1940, were the deeper justifications for these policies made explicit. It was assumed that as an activity, land-use planning should be administered by departments set up for that purpose: just as a local authority had an education department to provide education and a transport department to provide transport, a planning department should provide planning. The external environment, with which the plan was concerned, would change only slowly (or so it was assumed), so that periodic revisions of the plan—the 1947 Act specified every five years —would be enough to incorporate the changes that did occur.

A first modification of this view came about 1960. It was first observable in large-scale transportation studies, which demanded an expertise different from that of traditionally-trained planners; it then extended to comprehensive structure planning of large areas. Essentially the contribution made in these studies lay in four interrelated new developments: precise, quantified measurements of the relationships between the elements in an urban system, with an attempt to predict the interdependencies into the future; systematic generation of plan alternatives; evaluation of these alternatives, in exact form as far as possible, as a basis for choice of the final preferred plan; and a view of planning as a process of constant iteration and adjustment. At least two of these required new sets of techniques: simulation modelling of urban development was accompanied by cost-benefit techniques of all kinds.

This phase was pioneered in the United States first by the transportation planners from the Detroit and Chicago transportation studies of the middle 1950s, and then by early work in urban simulation, like the studies of Chaplin and Lowry, in the early 1960s. The transportation techniques were first applied in Britain on a large scale in the London Transportation Study from 1961, while simulation was only applied significantly after 1967, in sub-regional studies like Leicester–Leicestershire and in research projects such as those at the Centre for Environmental Studies, Cambridge and Reading. In this view of planning, the objectives were still viewed in terms of spatial arrangements; the techniques were developed precisely in order to generate a greater variety of quantified spatial patterns and then to choose systematically among them. Still ignored, for the most part, were questions of the relationship of physical planning to other sorts of planning. Land-use planning, though now integrated with transportation planning, was still viewed as a self-contained activity. The high point in the official acceptance of this view was probably Lady Sharp's report of January 1970, 'Transport Planning—the Men for the Job'.[1] Administratively the logical expression of this viewpoint is the integrated department of transportation and planning, as was established in the Greater London Council in 1969. Educationally, as suggested in the Sharp Report, the expression is common education of physical and transportation planners.

A second and more fundamental shift of outlook can be dated from about 1967. It appears to have had two very different origins. One was the attempt, first made in American defence planning at the time of Robert McNamara, to achieve greater cost effectiveness through the identification of objectives. As was first evident in McNamara's re-organization of the American defence effort, the result of this approach is radical administrative re-organization. Instead of divisions defined in terms of inputs (army, navy, air force) there is a centralized attempt to define objectives and the best ways of achieving them: the objectives themselves (for instance, greater capacity

---

[1] Lady Sharp, *Transport Planning: The Men for the Job*, H.M.S.O., London, 1970.

to deal with surprise nuclear attack) are in fact outputs of the system. Applied eventually to civil administration, this suggests a scrapping of traditional service-providing departments (transport department to supply transport, planning department to supply planning) and their replacement by a central planning activity which defines the objectives of the organization and alternative ways of achieving them. Even if the former service-providing departments are allowed to exist for administrative convenience, the point is that they will no longer enjoy the same autonomy as in the past.

The second and decisive impetus towards this style of planning comes in the United States with the associated crises of the urban ghetto and the Vietnam war. Planners there became convinced that national resources were being misapplied, first in terms of defence *versus* civil expenditure as a whole, and secondly in terms of the allocation of civil expenditure. Many planners became disillusioned with spatial planning as an objective in itself, stressing rather the social, aspatial content of planning, and in particular the different groups of the population which planning might help or benefit.

Spatial planning, critics were not slow to argue, might at worst actually benefit the well-off and penalize the poor, or at least be of no significance or interest to the poor. This emphasis on disaggregation of costs and benefits was in sharp contrast to the evaluative methods of the previous phase, which often tended to be highly aggregative and to assume, with classical economics, that the pleasures and pains of individuals were all to be ranked equally. Clearly the parallel between American and British experience here is far from close. British physical planners are far from experiencing the disillusionment of their American colleagues. Nor did they ignore social issues. But latterly, influenced by the American debate, they have become far more conscious that more physical planning decisions have social implications—sometimes complex and unexpected ones. Ironically, at the same time American planners have become disillusioned by the failure of PPBS in urban affairs to live up to its promises; see, for example, Moynihan.[1] But that is

---

[1] Daniel P. Moynihan, 'The role of the social scientist in action research', *Social Science Research Council Newsletter*, **10**, p. 5, 1970.

probably due to poor application rather than inherent weakness.

These two sets of influences interacted to produce a very different style of planning. It conceives of planning no longer as restricted to physical or spatial planning, but as a total process involving every aspect of public management. Planning in this view is concerned with relationship between *goals*, *objectives and targets*, on the one hand, and *public policy instruments* on the other. A public authority, such as a large city or a regional government, has a great variety of possible goals and objectives defined in different ways which may be wholly or partly incompatible. It certainly has a great variety of policy instruments, usually defined in terms of agencies. In the past, the argument runs, policy objectives were defined simply in terms of the activity of the agency: a transport department provided transport, a housing authority provided housing. The new planning views these merely as *inputs*, in terms of potentially available resources, for the production of *outputs* which are defined as the achievement of the objectives. Thus the transport department may help in achieving accessibility to jobs and services, mobility in a social as well as a geographical sense, and better living conditions (through accessibility to a greater variety of housing types within a given price range). Other agencies, for instance the housing agency, may provide whole or partial alternatives for achieving the same objectives. David Donnison's typical urban family with a housing problem, for instance, can solve their problem in various ways—many of them unrelated to the direct provision of housing. The task of the public authority is first to determine, analyse and order the objectives; second to consider the most efficient or economic way in which the policy instruments can contribute to achieving these objectives.

It is important to notice here that in most cases, both objectives and policy instruments will have spatial and aspatial aspects. This is clear from Alan Wilson's check list (Chapter Three). If we take as an objective the provision of *efficient and democratic ways of government*, for instance, efficiency and democracy may be promoted or hampered by the spatial arrangements of settlement and of local government units, though little is known on the question. Another objective, *income and income distribution*, may be affected by spatial arrangements very strongly, as David Donnison suggests.[1] But equally, it is clear that other policies of an aspatial nature can contribute to more equitable arrangements.

This new style of planning is applicable to any type of large complex public authority with a wide range of administration responsibilities, at whatever level of government. In so far as it applies to local government, it has been given official encouragement in the Report of the Maud Committee on Management in Local Government, in 1968, and has been embraced by a number of local authorities, as described by Brian McLoughlin in Chapter Five. In them, decisions are divided into policy making and detailed execution. Policy decisions are made by a small cabinet of committee chairmen, paralleled by a small committee of chief officers. They are essentially defined in terms of outputs of services representing the achievement of goals, as outlined by McLoughlin. Execution of these decisions is still devolved to agency departments. At the same time, the earlier revolution in planning style is also being reflected officially in the 1968 Planning Act, which calls on local planning departments to produce structure plans with an emphasis on the integration of land-use and transportation planning, systematic generation and evaluation of alternatives, and continuous monitoring and updating. Potentially, the two structures thus generated are capable of being linked into a powerful decision-making apparatus; spatial or physical planning has been revivified, rather than the reverse, by being placed within the wider framework of comprehensive strategic planning. But exactly how this is done is still far from clear to most local authorities.

It has been necessary to describe these changes in the recent past in order to speculate on changes in the near future. Clearly, the pace of intellectual and administrative change is accelerating, and the gap between one and the other seems to be narrowing. A planner trained in 1930 would have been reasonably at home in the planning office of 1960. The same cannot be said for the planner trained in 1960 who finds himself in the planning office of 1970. Consequently it is much more

---

[1] David Donnison, 'Liberty, Equality and Fraternity', *Three Banks Review*, **88**, pp. 20–21, 1970.

difficult than it was to predict twenty or thirty years ahead. Difficult as it is to make predictions about the future shape of the external environment, it is much more difficult to predict the shape of the ideas which will affect the planners' response. All that can be done is to attempt some speculations.

The most important of these is that recent developments have been largely induced by available computer technology and that they have been borrowed by urban planning from other areas, chiefly defence. We must suppose that this trend will continue and accelerate. The capacity of the planner to accept, digest and process information will be many times greater in 1980 than it is in 1970. By 2000 the explosion in capacity may be almost unimaginable. At the same time, we should suppose that in a sense computer technology will become simpler. The need for elaborate programming languages will probably have been eliminated. Direct interrogation of the computer—and conversely, direct interrogation of the people by the computer—will be feasible. Data will have become much richer because they will be more easily and directly comparable. It will be possible to explore consequences, choices and preferences in ways that are hardly possible now. The new capacity, if past experience is any guide, will itself generate new areas of interest.

Major Future Developments: Forecasting

From this, and treating the problem in its most general terms, it is possible to predict some of the likely main areas of development in the methodology of planning. They seem to be three in number.

The first concerns work on the external environment (not merely the physical environment, but the economic and social environment) within which the planner works, and which he seeks to manipulate and change. The main contributions here have come, and will come, from cybernetics, systems analysis, and the techniques of long- and medium-range forecasting. A particular tool, which will surely be developed, is the whole family of mathematical models of urban and regional growth and change, at various levels of disaggregation. At present these are mainly of an economic or spatial-economic type. These will be further developed, particularly through work on basic employment forecasting (which, in many exercises in urban modelling at present, is taken as 'given' from exogenous sources) and through work on disaggregated spatial interaction models which try to distinguish different patterns of spatial behaviour among different groups of the population. Such work may be expected increasingly to focus on a problem which now, because of lack of data, is avoided: the behavioural underpinnings of the models. To break away from simple mechanistic assumptions about causation, researchers may try increasingly to inject psychological and sociological theory and observation.

More work will undoubtedly be done, also, on relationships between different forecasts and different predictive models. At present, separate forecasts are made by separate agencies for different purposes; yet there is no systematic attempt to relate them. There is little sensitivity testing of the effect of bad forecasts on other dependent forecasts. Physical planning in the past has been particularly prone to take its basic predictions from other professions uncritically, with sometimes unfortunate results.

Major Future Developments: Objectives and Evaluation

The *second* main area of development will come in the analysis of the goals and objectives of planning, against which alternative outcomes are evaluated. Goal setting and evaluation have been difficult enough even in areas where some basic goals were not in question (such as defence). It is infinitely more difficult where the objectives of planning are multiple and even contradictory. At the same time, the problem has been complicated by a certain limited injection of democracy into the planning process, with the result that it is no longer possible to believe (as it was, perhaps, a decade ago), in a simple consensus among the public on the objectives of planning. The process may not go so far as in a more pluralist society like the United States; nevertheless it is possible that planning in Britain will be faced increasingly by conflicts of principle and of interest.

In answer to this problem, there appear to be two alternative responses. One holds that it is possible to investigate preferences by systematic interrogation of samples of the population. This would use the type of branching logic already employed in teaching machines and medical diagnostic tests, coupled with a game-playing technique whereby players used simulated resources (for instance, checkers representing money), to support their preferences, as outlined by Hoinville.[1] An approach of this sort assumes that people are capable of making rational consumer choices—whether among public services or among consumer goods. The opposing school denies this possibility. It suggests that the right way would be to extend the techniques of persuasion now so well understood by marketing experts in the private sector, so as to 'sell' public goods and services to the public. According to this school, any attempt to isolate 'rational' choice is an illusion; but by allowing public goods to compete for consumer support on the same basis as private goods, society would obtain some approximate notion of what people as a whole wanted. Both these approaches, in 1970, are in their infancy; the second hardly exists save as a thought.

In either case, there would need to be a development of physical simulation of future situations which might arise from the adoption of different public policies. The first approach would try to make this simulation as value-free, as objective and as emotionally neutral as possible. The second would not have to trouble about that, but would adopt the same techniques of persuasion—overt or hidden—as were already employed in marketing for the private sector. But in either case, it seems certain that there will be a systematic attempt to make concrete the consequences of public policies, which in their original form are too abstract for easy public comprehension.

The problem of evaluation cannot be separated from that of goal and objective setting. Pure aggregative cost-benefit analysis, as used in some major planning studies of the 1960s, did make the separation by assuming that objectives were irrelevant: it assumed that costs and benefits could be derived in the way that is conventionally used in cost-benefit analysis, that is by direct observation of people's preferences as revealed in their behaviour as producers and consumers. But as Peter Self has argued powerfully, this assumption is not logically good; for

---

[1] Gerald Hoinville, 'Evaluating Community Preferences', *Environment and Planning*, **3**, 33–50, 1971.

cost-benefit analysis is manifestly not derived from actual behaviour.[1] Further, since the valuations are based on the existing distribution of income, they are open to the objection that they systematically favour the rich at the expense of the poor. For this reason, there has been much interest in a deliberately disaggregated style of cost-benefit analysis—such as Lichfield's Planning Balance Sheet—where the elements are left separate so that a political decision can be taken on their relative weighting.[2]

Alternatively, it is possible, as Hill[3] suggests, to use an analysis in terms of goal-achievement, which depends directly on a prior political decision as to the weights given to various objectives. In both cases, the political decision is made explicit and the problem of weighting, or trade-off, remains. Hence the importance of further work on this question.

The analysis of goals and objectives, and the analysis of evaluation methods, will, therefore, proceed hand in hand. Much more work will be done on the theory of goal formulation by abstraction, which will demand a union of ethics, logic, the mathematics of operational research, political science and welfare economics. At the same time, empirical work will be done by students versed in the techniques of experimental psychology (particularly game-playing), welfare economics and market research. An alternative empirical approach will specifically use the techniques of marketing. The two approaches, the theoretical and the empirical, will obviously interact. But they will do so across a wide area of human choice. The work could not, and will not, be restricted to that narrow area of decision called physical or spatial planning.

Major Future Developments: Decision-Making

The *third* main area of development concerns the decision processes themselves, particularly in complex situations where

---

[1] Peter Self, 'Nonsense on Stilts: Cost Benefit Analysis and the Roskill Commission', *The Political Quarterly*, **41**, pp. 249–60, 1970.

[2] Nathaniel Lichfield, 'Evaluation methodology of urban and regional plans: a review', *Regional Studies*, **4**, (2), pp. 151–65, 1970.

[3] Morris Hill, 'A Goals-Achievement Matrix for evaluating Alternative Plans', *Journal of the American Institute of Planners*, **34**, pp. 19–29, 1968.

future outcomes are often in doubt. Here the main contributions have come from mathematical logic applied to operational research, and again they were applied first to quite different problems than the ones now under discussion. The important application to strategic planning problems of local authorities came as late as 1969, in the pioneer work of Friend and Jessop.[1] It is worth quoting their summary of the state of progress in developing 'a technology of strategic choice, based on a range of analytical techniques, some of which are themselves only in an embryonic state of development':

Method of finding solutions
Analysis of Interconnected Decision Areas (AIDA)
Other Systematic Design Method (e.g. Alexander)
Mathematical Programming

Methods of expressing preferences
Various Models for Simulation of Complex Social Systems
Cost-Benefit Analysis
Decision and Value Theory

Methods of exposing latent uncertainties
Sensitivity Analysis
Risk Analysis with explorations of assumptions through structural block diagrams

Methods of selecting exploratory actions
Cost Effectiveness Concepts

Methods of selecting immediate commitments
Analysis of Robustness of Action Sets

Some of these techniques apply to areas already discussed, and are borrowed from other disciplines. But the important central ones for the actual art of decision are those concerned with finding solutions, exposing uncertainties and selecting immediate commitments; they are derived from Friend and

---

[1] J. K. Friend and W. N. Jessop, *Local Government and Strategic Choice*, Tavistock, London, 1969.

Jessop's own work, which occurred at the margin of operational research and management science.

The basic assumptions underlying this approach are not easy, at first sight, to combine with those of the general forecasting approach outlined earlier. The idea of decision-making in uncertainty assumes essentially that the long-term future is unknown and that the strategy lies in accommodating to that fact. One major question for research is what combination of the methods is necessary or desirable or possible. It may well be that the Friend–Jessop approach will be progressively more important for those areas where the forecast outcome is very hazy.

In this area as in others so far discussed, the necessary research covers a wide area of human choice. It appears that planning is a general activity; the techniques relevant to it are relevant, in some measure, to all parts of it. Particular types of planning may require particular emphasis on particular techniques or applications; that is all. This will continue to be true in the future as in the recent past, but with an acceleration of the trends observed during the 1960s. Highly sophisticated research will increasingly be used as the basis of planning decisions, and the underpinnings will come from a variety of interrelated social and mathematical sciences—among them economics, geography, sociology, experimental psychology, cybernetics and operational research. There will be creative conflict between the approaches of different social sciences, or even between different schools within the same science. Solid research ability will become a prerequisite for many higher-level planning jobs, as has long been the case in industry and has recently become true in large planning offices like the Greater London Council. Arguments between professionals about priorities will have to be conducted in a common language, and this will become increasingly difficult as specialization proliferates.

The Relation to Planning Education

It has been necessary to make this long analysis of present achievements and future developments, in order to judge fairly the present state of development planning education. What is immediately clear is that this education is lagging behind the likely needs of professional planners even now; for the future, the gap may be even more serious.

Cynthia Cockburn has well illustrated the problem by distinguishing three stages of evolution in the definition of the planner's job; they correspond precisely to the analysis at the beginning of this chapter. In the first, planning is viewed simply as 'town planning'; it is done by Chartered Town Planners with help from contributors. In the second, planning becomes 'spatial planning', it involves the co-operation of a number of specialists among whom the planner is only one. He may be the design specialist in the team or he may—this has been the argument of the Royal Town Planning Institute—be the leader of the team through his capacity to synthesize. The argument about 'spatial planning' has racked the Institute throughout most of the 1960s, but now it has been overtaken by yet a third concept of planning: 'comprehensive strategic planning'. In this, there are a number of planning areas corresponding approximately to the provision of local authority services: educational planning, social services planning, housing planning, transport planning, and so on. Each has aspatial and spatial aspects. Clearly the Chartered Planner has no special competence to lead a team of such planners—though he may aspire to compete on equal terms with them for the top posts. As Cynthia Cockburn puts it:

> If the Royal Town Planning Institute were to attempt to be a relevant institution for the purposes of comprehensive, rather than only spatial, planning, it would imply a change in policy and structure far beyond that which was considered and rejected in 1965. There is some question whether a learned society might not serve such an interpretation of planning better than a professional body in the established sense, with a standard-setting and qualifying rôle.[1]

On the other hand, if the so-called town planner does not make this attempt, he will be reduced at best to one of a team, probably under the leadership of someone trained in another field. Yet the ironic situation is that the skills needed by this

---

[1] Cynthia Cockburn, *Opinion and Planning Education*, Centre for Environmental Studies Information Paper, CES IP 21. C.E.S., London, p. 67, 1970.

leader—and indeed by each member of the team, if they are to communicate adequately with each other—are probably not being taught anywhere; no qualification exists in them. The best succinct description of these new skills is 'urban management', and undoubtedly the closest parallel is with existing management education rather than with existing planning education. Certainly, most existing planning courses have only the most tenuous and partial relationship to what is now required. The re-orientation that would be needed is quite possibly beyond the capacity of the profession or the planning schools.[1]

Faced with this situation, the most helpful approach is probably to define the content of planning education in ideal terms, and then to consider how existing planning education could be adapted to it.

Three Stages of Education

The first point to be made is that, for the future, planning education will need to be based on a good general grounding in certain basic disciplines: mathematical logic, cybernetics, political science and welfare economics. The training in these subjects may well stress their application to practical problems of the modern world, but it will not be centrally vocational or practical in character: it will be disciplinary, conferring techniques of analysis, the capacity for logically rigorous thought, and basic languages, such as those of mathematics. Curiously, therefore, the basic training of the planner will be generalist; but in a quite different sense from the generalist planning of the past. The parallel is with that classically based education, which the public schools and Oxbridge provided for the aspiring nineteenth-century public administrator: a modern equivalent of Greats at Jowett's Balliol. Such a training could and should be common to the future industrial manager, the future civil servant and the future spatial planner. Indeed, since the training at this level would not be vocational, there would be no need at all for career decisions to be made. But particular interests or aptitudes could be met by specializations within

---

[1] Cockburn (*ibid.*) p. 177.

C

the broad course content. Those who were interested in spatial problems would take courses in geography and in urban economics, and perhaps in aspects of engineering. Those interested in social problems in an aspatial way would doubtless take courses in social psychology, sociology and politics. All of these would, however, need to stress a systems approach. The spatial system, the social system, the political system, would need to be illuminated and analysed in their complex inter-relationships.

For those concerned with social sciences, there is a particular and familiar enough problem. There is no easy correspondence between a student's *concern* with social and economic problems, and his *technical ability* to devise ways of solving them. Indeed, the mathematical intelligence which may be needed for the latter may be inimical to the involvement implied by the former. A central problem will be to lead students from the discussion of problems to the rigorous training needed to provide solutions. Training of this type would occupy the sixth form and undergraduate years. It would need to be based on a reform of teaching in some areas (particularly mathematics) which is already taking place. Fundamental theory in the social sciences would need to enter in the sixth form. Here, and in undergraduate courses, education would need to be more multi-disciplinary than now. The problem will be to avoid a half-baked hodge-podge. Assuming that Greats (and its equivalent, Modern Greats) could instil three basic disciplines, this would probably be the most that could be hoped for in their new equivalent. The new course in Scientific Bases of Planning in Reading, for instance, works on this principle by combining cybernetics, economics and geography. Other combinations could be offered within the same framework. But there would need to be some common approach and common content in the courses, which should consist in cybernetics and systems analysis. Branching within some of the subjects would allow a measure of specialism in the final under-graduate year. The student who was particularly interested in spatial aspects might develop his interest in urban geography and urban economics at that time; the intending industrial manager might specialize in social psychology and industrial sociology. It is unnecessary and undesirable to suggest a single fixed structure here. Some universities and polytechnics may prefer to keep a stronger department or disciplinary basis; others may develop more loosely-structured courses, with a greater variety of options.

Not all future planners would be trained in this way. Some might be trained in a scientific or technological mould, through a study of engineering. But hopefully, just as the student of Greats would have a grounding in cybernetics, so would the student of engineering have a basis in the understanding of social and economic systems. What is needed here is the development of mixed and structured courses—mixed in the sense that they straddle the traditional boundary of sciences and social sciences, structured in that they contribute to understanding of a well articulated set of problems.

The second level of training would be more specifically vocational. It would consist of intensive courses aimed to develop particular skills taught at immediate postgraduate level or possibly after one or two years on the job. In many cases they might be taught on an intensive, part-time or sandwich basis with practical work developed on the job itself. But in general, they would be equivalent in level to one- or two-year Master's degrees (by teaching) in universities today. They would train people to do junior management jobs with a large technical content, such as transportation planning, traffic management and control, structure planning or (to take other fields) educational planning, housing management or recreational planning. Some of the Master's courses in planning developed in the late 1960s, and conventionally labelled the 'new planning courses', are of this character, as are courses in related fields such as traffic engineering. It is assumed that such courses will greatly extend in range and scope, so that they will become a usual part of higher education. They will also become steadily more rigorous and demanding in their content of technical skills.

A student trained in this way, first through an undergraduate generalist course with a specific basis in systems thinking and then through a specialist technical course, should be well fitted for his chosen job in central or local government or in various public planning agencies. He will have chosen technical skill together with an ability to communicate with other professionals in a variety of problems, and in a number of different groups, which he may encounter. At one time or another, for instance, the transportation planner in a local authority will need to communicate with his opposite numbers in railway and 'bus management, the police, structure planners, housing managers and planners, recreation planners and a number of other similar specialists in local and central government. The essential point is that all should be able to communicate in a reasonably common language—a style of analysis and decision-taking. They will also need a common understanding of the needs and the attitudes of their client publics—an understanding which has come much later to the physical planner than to his colleagues as housing, education or race relations.

This will be sufficient for junior management, and it is at this level that a great deal of the technical innovation will take place. (Witness, for instance, the history of land-use/transportation planning, where much of the development was carried through by personnel under thirty-five years of age.) But higher-level management posts—the directors of major service departments in local authorities, for instance—will probably require additional training in the problems of large-scale co-ordination and strategic planning that are involved. At the same time, because of the speed of innovation, they may themselves need re-orientation in the more basic technical skills. I.B.M., for instance, have argued that their personnel will become technologically obsolete every fifteen years or so, and will need complete retraining. This suggests a need for special high-level courses in urban management, coupled with intensive refresher versions of the more junior technically-based courses. Such courses will probably be short-term and intensive in character, on the lines of the work developed at many business and trade schools. It is unlikely that people at this level would spare their time, or that their employers would spare it for them, for very long. On the other hand, because of their job experience, they should have a faster level of take-up of the new information and skills than the average student. Re-education may become as large as, or larger than, first education; we try to quantify the point at the end of this chapter.

These three levels of training—the undergraduate generalist, the postgraduate vocational, and the post-experience managerial—are imperfectly developed today. At the undergraduate level, vocational training in planning runs directly counter to the ideas expressed here, and has no part in the scheme; but few interdisciplinary courses of the type required seem to be developing. There is a particular danger that the rapid expansion of social science courses, which has been observable since 1965, may be accompanied by dilution in the rigour of the training, particularly where this involves a strong mathematical element. New undergraduate courses of a more rigorous kind are, therefore, one priority, and they will pose some of the biggest challenges of organization and co-ordination to those who teach them. At the postgraduate level, the problems are probably fewer: a number of courses already exist, though most have developed since 1965; it is easier to identify the lines of future growth, and the vocational objective of each course is more easily defined. The biggest problems of all probably occur at the post-experience level, because of the lack of precedents for such courses in the sphere of public administration. Questions like the frequency and duration of the courses, their residential basis, the right age and experience of the participants, and the character of the work, are all equally unexplored. Some can be answered only by experience—which means making expensive mistakes.

Relationship to Royal Town Planning Institute Policy

The three-stage concept of education set out here was devised well before the publication, in December 1971, of the Royal Town Planning Institute discussion paper on the future of the planning profession.[1] Nevertheless, to a considerable degree it appears to fit the more radical reforms of the scope of the profession which are envisaged there.

Essentially the discussion paper argues that if a change is to be made in order to widen the present restricted base of entry to the profession, there are three main possibilities. The least radical would be to open up the profession to all those engaged in planning the physical environment, including specialists like transportation planners, to create an Institute of Environmental Planning. The second would bring in social and economic planners, to create an Institute of Community

---

[1] Royal Town Planning Institute, *Town Planners and their Future: A Discussion Paper*, The Institute, London, 1971.

Planning. The third and most radical would turn the Institute into a professional organization (an Institute of Planning) of corporate planners, or urban managers; though it is recognized that there would be no monopoly here. All these alternatives would imply some degree of specialization in professional qualification; henceforth members would no longer be, as they have been in the past, generalist planners able to turn their skills to any sort of job.

Broadly, the concept of education outlined in this chapter would allow certain sorts of specialism to be taught at postgraduate level, to people who had shared various types of preparatory undergraduate education. They could couple several of these courses, so as to acquire a group of related skills. And all the courses would necessarily involve a common element of basic principles of corporate planning. The higher level skills of urban management, together with refresher courses in the basic skills, would be taught to more senior professionals with several years of experience behind them. These people would have varied backgrounds, not all by any means in the area now covered by the examinations of the Royal Town Planning Institute. For common education in urban management would be given in common to educational planners, health planners and others—not merely to environmental planners, or environmental planners supplemented by economic and social planning specialists as envisaged in the Institute's second main option.

The basic problem, unresolved in the discussion document, is who or what is to decide the qualifications and the admission policy? In recent years, the Royal Town Planning Institute has seen whole professional areas grow up rapidly outside its scope, first in the sphere of transportation planning, then in economic planning, after that in social planning, and finally in corporate planning. The professionals now working in these fields are not usually Royal Town Planning Institute members, and many have alternative qualifications. It seems doubtful that the Royal Town Planning Institute could assert any effective monopoly of teaching or qualification in this field, as it has hitherto achieved in respect of its own examinations or the courses to which it has granted special exemption. It may find itself giving more or less automatic recognition to any course taught by a university or polytechnic, and thereby possessing suitable academic validation, in defined areas. The initiative would pass to the educators themselves, rather than to the mixture of academics and practitioners who have constituted the Royal Town Planning Institute's educational committee. But this runs up against the key sensitive issue in all professional education—which, perhaps, is specially acute in the Royal Town Planning Institute because of the wide fringe area it shares with related professions such as architecture and engineering.

Some Problems of Organization

One point can, however, be made with some confidence. At postgraduate and post-experience levels, many of the courses will take forms quite different from conventional university education: particularly short courses, sandwich courses and even day release courses. Most of the people taking them will probably be married, and many will have families. The great majority will be salaried posts. So organization and financial support will have to take new forms also. Organizationally, the courses will either have to be organized as short seminar-type courses, in which participants leave their families (a variant of this is the longer-type course organized on a Monday–Friday basis, with weekend release), or they will have to be organized on a daily 0900–1700 hours basis in major population centres where participants can commute, or there will have to be full family accommodation on campuses—a measure few universities in Britain seem yet to have faced up to. Financially, it will be unrealistic to imagine that participants will make heavy financial sacrifices to enter the courses; they will have too many fixed commitments for this, even if they were willing. Support will, therefore, need to come in the form of full salary support from employers, either as direct salary payments or scholarship funds. The first raises particular problems if the student wishes to change employer soon after taking the course—a common enough event, because of the additional qualification—and employers may well be deterred from supporting members of staff who may use the opportunity to leave. For this reason an open scholarship fund may be preferable.

Up to now, planning as a profession has been relatively slow to adjust to these needs: other professions, notably child care and public health practitioners, have had much more generous help in financing mid-career retraining. For child care, as early as 1948 the Home Office recognized the principle in its Children's Act by reserving a small percentage of grant money for training. And yet the widening and deepening of technical skills has been at least as great in planning as in the other professions. The inescapable conclusion is that many working planners are becoming intellectually and technically obsolescent, at a rapid pace.

In terms of academic organization, too, the new courses will present problems. Each of them will have various facets, some, but not all of which it will share with others. The resulting patterns can be usefully analysed in terms of mathematical sets. A postgraduate (or early post-experience) course in land-use transportation planning, for instance, has at least these facets: mainly spatial in character, engineering and social science based, with a strong mathematical content, leading to local authority work, an essential part of the total pattern of urban management. A similar course in structure planning has all these attributes except the engineering basis; it probably needs a stronger basis also in certain social sciences, particularly sociology. A course in social planning, linking physical planning and social services planning, would have these features: mainly aspatial in character, based sociology and political science (and probably economics), leading to local authority work, closely related both to educational and structural planning, an essential part of the total pattern of urban management. Given this variation, the question is, which type of academic umbrella would best shelter the different courses?

Here there are several possibilities. Traditionally, in many universities, course structures have been organized on *disciplinary* lines, represented by *faculties*: thus Letters, Social Sciences, Physical Sciences. This is appropriate to universities engaged mainly in undergraduate education, but becomes progressively less suitable as universities and polytechnics develop *interdisciplinary* postgraduate and post-experience work. There, the tendency is to develop schools based on the character of the *vocational interests*: thus a Graduate School of Business Studies, or a Graduate School of Urban Studies. Usually these sit, in rather uneasy fashion, within the faculty structure, though in fact many of their activities stretch naturally across faculty boundaries, requiring complex and time-consuming duplication or triplication of administrative arrangements. Unfortunately, also, the activities of many of these schools themselves overlap with each other. Output budgeting would naturally be taught in a business school, but is equally appropriate now to an urban school. There is considerable overlap between the content of planning education.

The way out of this dilemma is probably to accept the logical consequences of the classification of courses made in this chapter. Undergraduate courses should still be run in discipline-based faculties, though considerable flexibility in interpretation will be necessary there: the modern equivalent of 'Greats' described earlier would be a social science course, but includes elements not now normally taught as social science. Both postgraduate and post-experience courses should be organized within a Graduate School of Public Administration or Management (which might alternatively be called a Graduate School of Strategic Planning, if that term did not have an unfortunate ambiguity for the general public). Within this structure, the postgraduate courses would be in general more narrowly conceived within a vocational mould, and would require the assembly of a more limited range of skills than the broad-based post-experience courses. Increasingly, university or polytechnic teachers may have to be appointed jointly by undergraduate departments (or faculties) and by postgraduate schools.

Such a broad umbrella would permit a very wide range of courses—ranging from engineering-based to social science-based, from the highly spatial to the highly aspatial—to be taught as part of a common structure centred on the strategic planning function of the large public authority. The central style of the education would be managerial, but it would be applied specifically to the complex problems of public strategic planning, which are outside the usual range of management school or business school education. A university or polytechnic adopting such a school would presumably do so as an alternative to setting up an ordinary business school, not as an addition to it, so problems of overlap would not arise there.

Since this school would be engaged solely in professional education, its own degrees would presumably convey their own professional standing. Within a few years the demand for professionals trained in this way will become very pressing, and the supply will barely exist. If the argument is accepted that in the future professional competence will turn basically on academic competence applied in a particular field, there is every reason to allow the degree to stand as the badge of professional standing, without the need for further professional qualification, such as membership of an Institute of Public Administration. Given this argument, it is suggested that broadly such a school could establish qualifications at two levels. The first, or postgraduate level, would give a Master's degree which would certify professional competence in a particular area of public planning—such as educational planning, health planning, or land-use/transportation planning. This degree could be subject to periodic renewal, or 'updating', if required, by means of periodic refresher courses. (It offers the intriguing possibility that degrees be classed like vintages, with the oddity that, like Beaujolais, younger usually means better.) The post-experience degree might perhaps be as Doctorate, based principally on work for a dissertation done in the professional post itself—and original contribution to knowledge applied directly to the candidate's own work experience.

Thus the meaning of professionalism in planning will show a sharp change. Especially at the higher levels, planners will be generalists concerned with the job of urban management. They will be selected partly on the basis of their professional record, and partly on the basis of their academic achievements in relation to their professional work. There will be no single professional qualification to give entry to posts at this level, rather a variety of higher degrees given by universities or polytechnics through Schools of Public Administration, probably coupled with a variety of postgraduate qualifications from these same schools or from other places. The existing planning courses will presumably adjust to this new status; if they do not, they will soon find themselves relegated to a subordinate rôle in training people who will be the executors, rather than the makers, of decisions.

The Scale of the Need

During the 1960s there were repeated assertions about the shortage of trained planners; they were widely divergent, and appear to have been based on no very close study of actual manpower needs.[1] The University Grants Committee, in planning for the quinquennium 1967–72, accepted a high estimate: that the total size of the planning profession should be about 10 000. It therefore made funds available to expand up to this level by 1978, most of the increase being achieved by 1973. By 1970 it seemed likely that the output from Royal Town Planning Institute oriented courses alone could be as great as 1000 per year by the mid-1970s, with independent courses yielding another 400 qualified students a year. This, in turn, led to doubts whether the total output was not too great for the needs.

This question cannot be meaningfully answered without a close look at the purposes of planning education. The U.G.C. estimates were based on a fairly restrictive concept of a planner. They took no direct account, for instance, of the shortage of transport planners, where Lady Sharp's report indentified a need for 400–500 trained men for local government jobs in England outside London, with another 300–50 to meet the needs of London, Scotland, Ireland, Wales, central government, transport industries and consultants: a total of 700–850, to be built up over thirty years through courses with 100 or 200 a year.[2]

Further, the U.G.C. estimates took no account of the problem of retraining, both for land-use and transport planners. If the argument earlier in this chapter were right, it could mean a very great expansion in this field, perhaps eventually rivalling in scale the initial training of planners. If, for instance, 10 000 land-use planners and 1000 transport planners were to return for retraining for as little as three months (or the equivalent in short courses), every five years, this would be the equivalent of a throughput of 700 students per nine-month academic year. And this seems a fairly conservative estimate of the amount of retraining that will be needed in the future.

Lastly, the estimates took no account of the needs of comprehensive strategic planning (or, as it is widely coming to be known, urban management). This, at present, is hardly being taught at all. If it is to be taught, it will have to be provided not merely for land-use and transport planners, but for senior

---

[1] Cynthia Cockburn, *op. cit.*, 1970 (see p. 56).

[2] Lady Sharp, *op. cit.*, 1970, pp. 19–20.

officials from a variety of departments. If all intending senior officials and their immediate deputies took such courses (a fairly conservative assumption, perhaps, for the future), and if there were in future some seventy to eighty top tier authorities in Britain, each with an average of ten policy departments and a typical thirty-year career span in top posts from appointment to retirement, then perhaps the demand might be $\dfrac{80 \times 10 \times 2}{30}$, or about fifty a year. This takes no account of the need in central government or in special agencies, which could clearly inflate the demand to double or more this amount.

These qualifications merely underline the obvious point that the nature of the course is critical. Conventional courses in land-use planning may well have reached their ceiling and even gone above it: courses in transport planning and its relation to structure planning, in retraining planners, in urban management, and for retraining planners, certainly have not. The changing demands on professionals in the future will be expressed partly by changes in the content of existing courses, but more importantly by the development of entirely new qualifications. But these latter needs are particularly difficult to quantify. The only conclusion is that the need above all will be to maintain the maximum flexibility in organizing education for planners. There has never been a time in which ideas on the subject changed so rapidly; the most progressive course of 1960 would have been sadly outdated by 1970. Any attempt to put planning education in a straitjacket, whether in terms of conception or in terms of organization, is bound to fail. The losers will be first the students, and second the resulting profession.

Chapter Five

The Future of the Planning Profession

BRIAN MCLOUGHLIN

Introduction

In 1967 the government asked the Monopolies Commission to examine 'the general effect on the public interest of certain restrictive practices so far as they prevail in relation to the supply of professional services'. The resulting report was published recently,[1] and has reminded us once again that we live in a world of increasing professionalism where 'new and rapidly changing technologies are requiring new kinds of occupations and notable changes in old occupations. New organizational arrangements are exerting profound influences on the occupational order'.[2]

The planning profession arose almost sixty years ago in response to just those sorts of changes. It has grown very considerably in size since then. But its composition has also altered markedly, especially during the 1960s, so that there is now a sizeable minority of members who are 'pure' planners (without any other professional or academic allegiance) and social

---

[1] Monopolies Commission, 'A report on the general effect on the public interest of certain restrictive practices so far as they prevail in relation to the supply of professional services', Part 1 of the report, Cmnd. 4463, H.M.S.O., London, 1970.
[2] Howard M. Vollmer and Donald L. Mills (eds). *Professionalization*, Englewood Cliffs, N.J., Prentice-Hall, Inc., 1966.

scientists alongside the architects, surveyors and engineers who traditionally have dominated its ranks.

In recent years the Royal Town Planning Institute has become uncomfortably aware of the ways in which changes in its context affect the body corporate, and especially this was true of the membership 'crisis' of 1964–5. That adjustments to the currents of change involve not only the definition of membership—or *who* shall be allowed in—but also education in the widest sense, has been made abundantly clear by the work of Cockburn.[1] She rightly reminds us also that planners 'are by no means alone in their difficulty in finding an appropriate stance' and the resolution of problems about the future of the planning profession cannot be kept, as it were, within the family.

For problems of professions, professional people and professionalization are nothing less than an aspect of twentieth-century life, and one of increasing weight and importance. Although professional occupations now form an important minority of all jobs, by the turn of the century they may well form the majority. This could come about in three ways: by absolute growth in the numbers of people in existing professions; by the creation of new occupations which are professional in nature; and by the professionalization of occupations which are not now so organized or regarded.

The changes that have occurred in the structure of society as between the nineteenth and the twentieth centuries require evolution of new professional rôles and new concepts of professionalism. One of the most important changes is the decline of the amateur entrepreneur and his gradual replacement by professional managers from many different intellectual and disciplinary backgrounds. Another is the emergence of the mixed economy of the Welfare State which

> invests in services designed to shape, repair, and reshape the physical, intellectual, psychological, and social equipment of its citizens. The latter services have the capacity of changing on a

---

[1] Cynthia Cockburn, *Facts about planning courses*, C.E.S.-IP-14, London, Centre for Environmental Studies, 1970a; and: *The provision of planning education*, C.E.S.-IP-15, 1970b; *Opinion and planning education*, C.E.S.-IP-21, 1970c.

massive, organized scale the traditional characteristics of humanity itself and have been expanding at a great rate.[1]

The rise of professions has changed the effects they exert, not just quantitatively but also qualitatively, and now they are *reshaping the structure and purpose of organizations* on a far greater scale than in the nineteenth century. We make this point early on because it can provide a framework for much of the chapter. We shall make some considerable use of it in drawing conclusions about the planning profession.

We will have to consider changes in our conception of the nature of planning itself; various institutional changes including the structure of central government, local government, the creation of *ad hoc* agencies to carry out particular planning tasks and the development of research agencies; the growth of new styles of administration and management, especially in local government, and the changing types of mixes of skill that these will require. The profession will also be affected by developments in education, not only in courses 'recognized' by the Royal Town Planning Institute but also by educational developments in other closely-related academic and professional fields. Finally, as we have already said, the changing nature of professionalism and professional institutions will be bound to affect the planning profession and the Institute. One useful way of organizing such a discussion, and at the same time relating it to the previous book, is to adopt the threefold division of planning tasks proposed then by Wilson[2]—policy, analysis and design.

Local Government and the Future of the Profession

Among the more important long-term trends at work are the shift towards more explicit discussion of societal goals and objectives as they arise within or affect the administrative area concerned, the concomitant use of management tools such as PPB systems and their associated information and intelligence

---

[1] Eliot Friedson, Editorial Foreword, *American Behavioural Scientist*, 1970, pp. 467–74.
[2] Alan Wilson, 'Forecasting "planning"', in Peter Cowan (ed.), *Developing Patterns of Urbanisation*, Edinburgh, Oliver and Boyd, 1969, pp. 68–9.

systems, the use of operational measurements to compare objectives (or targets) with actual achievements, a greater emphasis on social, economic and physical outputs rather than on technical inputs, a more 'open' style of government in which consultation with client groups or their active participation is employed, and recognition of the need for flexibility within broad limits of policy.

Evidence of some of these trends is found in recent reports on the management and staffing of local government,[1] to which response has already started. The newer forms of management structure have several common features. The council itself (i.e. the elected and co-opted members) will have a policy group or 'cabinet' which will debate and resolve major issues of strategic policy. A small number of committees will deal mainly with the execution of policies in specific functional areas such as education, housing and personal services on a day-to-day basis.

The staffs of local authorities are likely to be grouped into a similar pattern, i.e. a 'management group' of chief officers will discuss and formulate major policies for consideration by the policy groups or council as a whole, while major groups of functional departments will be formed under the council's most senior officers. Such directors, together with the chief executive, are the management group of the authority's staff and form the counterpart of the 'cabinet' group of members. Strategic land-use and transport planning, detailed development design, traffic management and development control may be similarly affected. Lady Sharp has recommended that land-use and transport planning should be integrated within the remit of one senior officer in local government, and that the education of land-use and transport planners should go hand in hand.[2]

One essential feature of these changes is to distinguish between the formulation and review of strategic policies on the one hand and their detailed execution and implementation on the other. A distinction is being drawn between the building of

---

[1] Ministry of Housing and Local Government, *The Management of Local Government* (*2 Vols*) H.M.S.O., London, 'The Maud Report', 1967; also: Ministry of Housing and Local Government. *The Staffing of Local Government*, H.M.S.O., London, 'The Mallaby Report', 1967.

[2] Lady Sharp, *Transport Planning: the Men for the Job*. H.M.S.O., London, 1970.

houses and housing policies, between equipment for schools and educational policies; between local planning programmes and 'green space' policies. This is also reflected in the 1968 and 1971 Planning Acts (1969 in Scotland) which call for policy-orientated 'structure plans' and problem-orientated 'action areas'.

The traditional orientation of the planning profession towards a comprehensive, long-range, welfare-orientated view of the world, fits very readily into the policy-making level at which the interactions between various facets of urban-regional life are debated and certain conflicts are resolved. The profession's particular contribution at this level of debate would be to spell out the urban-form implications of alternative policy bundles, and the physical opportunities and constraints which might operate on them. But also, the planner 'has a role to play in the selection of general overall goals for the social, economic and physical development of the area'. He will be able to 'produce information on existing conditions, the available alternative opportunities and the consequences of selecting certain groups of goals'. These activities would be part and parcel of a general interdisciplinary service in the policy formulation posts of top management. In addition, planners could help as individuals with a particular skill 'to reach solutions in a physical situation in response to social and economic factors'.[1]

At the level of implementation, the profession's traditional physical-design basis would seem to be relevant in helping with the implementation of policies at the local scale where development and construction were involved. At both levels, however, several different kinds of skill would be needed. For example, at the policy level, social science and financial skills must be mixed with development skills, and at the level of local execution, architects, engineers, welfare, education, housing and legal skills would be needed in amalgamation.

Although the profession has had this traditional concern for comprehensiveness, and a long-range view, it has hitherto been dominated by the methods of physical and spatial design. The

---

[1] Royal Town Planning Institute, 'The Changing Shape of the Planning Process', on R.T.P.I. discussion note. R.T.P.I., London, 1970; Royal Town Planning Institute. *Town Planners and their Future*, a discussion note, R.T.P.I., London, 1971.

policy-making realms of local government are now adopting the 'planning method'[1] of corporate management in which uncertainty is freely admitted and conflicts resolved in more subtle and incremental ways. While the intellectual style needed to cope with such situations is commonly found in the social and management sciences and in operational research, it is new to the planning profession.[2]

The planning profession, therefore, like many others, will have to become accustomed to, and equipped for, working in very flexible arrangements with people of other skills. Although social scientists have worked in planning departments for a considerable time, their efforts have typically been used to provide inputs to land-use design exercises at all scales. The inter-departmental task forces will tend to seek out the most appropriate strategies for each particular problem encountered; in some cases, physical design solutions may predominate; in others, the best course of action may not involve any physical changes at all.

These aspects of the future local governments will require changes of the profession. Peter Hall's plea for some kind of new 'planning Greats' will be echoed in policy-making circles. Along the corridor where detailed execution and implementation is done, the stage could be set for some sharp boundary warfare between planners and architects in particular. The vexed questions of education, professional skills and loyalties in the field of 'urban design' are still unresolved and could be exacerbated in action area task forces.

In nineteenth-century models of the firm and the public office, clear cut 'vertical' departments are defined in relation to *inputs* (bus trips, houses) and require definable skills and techniques (P.S.V. drivers, architects). Professional solidarity and mystique reinforce departmentalism, because although there are some problems interdepartmentally, everyone within any department can communicate most readily with his immediate colleagues.

The new models of organization require that skills be com-

---

[1] Peter Hall, *Theory and Practice of Regional Planning*, London, Pemberton Books, 1970.

[2] John K. Friend and W. N. Jessop, *Local Government and Strategic Choice*, Tavistock Publications, London, 1969.

bined and recombined in different mixes in relation to *output* requirements of both broad policy and specific problem-solving. These mixes depend upon an openness of mind, specific knowledge, positive attitudes towards multi-disciplinary working and, above all, some common language in which to discuss urban-regional systems and problems.

As departmentalism and technique-orientated work gives way to problem-orientated task-force and policy-grouping methods, so, too, professionalism will have to adapt.

Analytical Power and the Profession in the Future

The technical skills and procedures available to planning in practice have increased greatly in both range and depth in recent years. At one time these were confined to physical design expertise, but to this has been added demographic, economic and geographical techniques of increasing sophistication. Latterly we have seen the application of operations research and management science methods to planning. Many of these applications have been greatly augmented by increased computer power and capacity.

Application of these new powers and skills is made to the planning effort in two ways. Firstly, people possessing such skills are employed in planning agencies of all kinds, and although they are few at present, their numbers seem to be increasing (if advertisements for jobs are any guide). Secondly, a number of professional planners acquire at least the rudiments of such skills, or their methods of approach, via the appropriate literature, conferences, seminars and, to a very small but growing degree, by attending mid-career training courses.

Over the years the R.T.P.I. has tried in several ways to adapt to these developments. In the 1950s its entry requirements were altered to make it easier for economists, geographers and sociologists to join the Institute. In 1964 the council tried to alter the membership policy to admit such people directly, but failed, and personalities closely associated with this move were 'sacked' at the 1965 elections.[1] The new final examination syllabus (1968–9) of the Institute attempts to diversify planning

---

[1] Cynthia Cockburn, *op. cit.* 1970c, pp. 54–81.

on the basis of a generalist qualification with four, largely spatial, options. If it is accepted that the traditional physical, spatial-design element of planning is not experiencing any rapid growth, while those other elements of needed skills are, then it seems that the R.T.P.I. must become representative of a smaller and smaller fraction of planning's intellectual base.

People educated in these other disciplines—social, management and operational research sciences—may well belong to a professional body, but the institutions themselves and members' relationships with them (and with employers) may often be very different from those of the R.T.P.I. and planners. For example, membership of the Institute of British Geographers, the Operational Research Society, the Computer Society or the British Sociological Association is usually irrelevant as far as employment and promotion within local government planning departments is concerned. But membership of the R.T.P.I. is a critical factor in advancement beyond the junior levels, and often people with social-science and other skills will have to undergo the whole of the 'generalist' R.T.P.I. final examination simply to make progress in the planning office rather than aspiring to a professional commitment to planning as a vocation. The demand for planning education may be falsely inflated by such candidates. So too may the demand for Chartered Town Planners in planning agencies as long as they insist on advertising for a 'planning assistant' when what they really want is an economic geographer or a systems analyst. There are some indications that social, operational research and management scientists have been more widely used and have been able to make a fuller contribution to planning outside the normal local government agencies—e.g. central government, research bodies, *ad hoc* planning teams and private practices. It may be that this is so because of the absence of those barriers which hold back non-R.T.P.I. members in local government and the positive encouragement of a variety of contributions in a truly multi-disciplinary fashion.

'Design' and the Profession in the Future

It should be emphasized that 'design' is used in a wide sense to mean all those processes which generate possible courses of action, whether of a long-range and strategic or shorter-range and detailed nature.[1] Strategic planning in the future will involve explicit discussion of goals and objectives, the generation and testing of alternatives, the admission of uncertainty, and the monitoring and evaluation of outcomes along several welfare dimensions, and will make such 'design' activity very different from the 'master planning' of the past. The mental agility and dynamism necessary for this work, the awareness of political possibility, the ability to generate ideas and to communicate with colleagues in a common language of 'strategic choice'[2] will not be guaranteed by membership of any particular professional body. Certainly, deep understanding of some aspects of urban-regional systems will be necessary, but this is produced largely by the interplay of higher education, personality and experience. The uncertainty of a rapidly changing world must be faced in the processes of plan formulation, and it will be necessary to strive for 'flexibility in the form of plans which are hedging bets against unknown contingencies'.[3]

At present these attitudes to urban government are somewhat exceptional, but we might hazard an informed guess that within ten years most planners will find themselves working (or seeking employment) in authorities who have adopted what is called 'comprehensive strategic planning'[4] and which comprises 'both non-spatial and space-related considerations. It is the planning function of the entire local authority and surpasses the rôle of the planning department altogether'. In such situations 'the Chartered Planner, as head of the planning department (in the spatial sense) is no more than one of several kinds of planner. He may well be "synthesizing" a part of the planning process. He is certainly not synthesizing all of it. . . . He has no possibility at all of sustaining, by virtue of education or of professional membership, a right to lead a team that contains an educational planner, a social development planner, a recreational planner, etc. He may, however, devise a unique rôle within the team and become *one* of those who can aspire to its leadership. But what happens to spatial planning once

---

[1] Alan Wilson, 'Models in Urban Planning: a Synoptic Review of Recent Literature, *Urban Studies*, **5**, pp. 249–76, 1968.

[2] Friend and Jessop, *op. cit.*

[3] Alan Wilson, *op. cit.*

[4] Cockburn, *op. cit.*, p. 53.

strategic planning receives organizational shape will remain to be seen'.

Designs at the strategic level imply detailed programmes of action—physical, social, and economic—at the level of the environment, the localized frame of reference for daily life shown up by recent research.[1] Here, at the grass roots, there will be equally vexing problems of interdisciplinary working, mostly concerning common languages in which to communicate objectives, and problem-solving methods. Similar sorts of mental qualities will be needed here as at the strategic level, but in addition some 'harder' professional skills will be indispensable. Detailed plans for action areas and associated local programmes will call for professional abilities in community development, education, housing, law, public finance, personal welfare and health, race relations, traffic and civil engineering, architecture, landscape design and so on. The main qualification for membership of such task forces (whether in industry or in government, practice or research) is the ability to make some rather specific contribution. The big questions for professional planners are—what will this contribution be? and is it likely to be sufficiently different from that of other disciplines?

Professions and Professionalism

One of the fullest and most useful studies of professionalism is that of Millerson[2] in which he defines a profession as a 'type of higher-grade non-manual occupation, with both subjectively and objectively recognized status, possessing a well-defined area of study or concern and providing a definite service, after advanced training and education' (p. 10).

Professional organizations have a number of primary functions which include those of:

> qualifying;
> organizing;
> studying and communicating;
> registering the competent;
> promoting high standards of conduct.

---

[1] Royal Commission on Local Government in England. Research Studies, *Community Attitudes Survey*, vol. 9, H.M.S.O., London, 1969.
[2] Millerson, *The Qualifying Associations*, Routledge and Kegan Paul, London, 1964, pp. 28–32.

They also have secondary functions of raising professional status, controlling entry, protecting the professional and the public, acting as pressure groups, organizing social functions and carrying out welfare and benevolent work among members and their dependents (pp. 28–32).

Millerson recognized four main types of professional organization—the *prestige* organization (e.g. Royal Society), the *occupational* association (e.g. the Society of County Treasurers, the British Medical Association), the *study* association (e.g. the Institute of British Geographers) and the *qualifying* association (the R.I.B.A., R.I.C.S., R.T.P.I.) The main advantages of belonging to a qualifying association are, first and foremost, possession of the qualification itself which demonstrates achievement and gives access, sometimes uniquely, to job opportunities; secondly, membership may bring services which are not otherwise available and contact with other people working in the field.

He goes on to point out that if these latter services (e.g. library, meetings, conferences, seminars, specialized publications, information) are weakly developed, then loyalty to the institution becomes limited to its value in giving the qualification as a 'job ticket'.

It is obvious that a major characteristic of twentieth-century professionalism is the swing away from the older dominance of private practice and fee-paying clients towards salaried employment, very often in the public services. This trend is deep-seated and likely to continue. Where a large proportion of the membership of a profession are in salaried employment, institutional forms based on private practice (fees, code of conduct, etc.) may appear less and less relevant as this trend continues. Other dilemmas may also appear. For if an association becomes predominantly concerned with giving qualifications—with technique, study and education—it may find itself rendered superfluous by the long-term trend in many fields towards academic education for professional subjects. At first, academic training is the exception, but it gradually becomes complementary to professional examinations and finally may substitute for them almost entirely.

Independent professionals (i.e. those working for clients) understandably try to establish a monopoly of practice. But professional people in salaried employment typically 'have not obtained, and probably could not obtain such a monopoly position. They are employed in a wide variety of jobs (and) the determination of the type of work they do is in the hands not of themselves, nor of the professional association, but of the employer. The relationship . . . is very different from that between practitioner and client. Professional monopoly is designed to protect the client from the incompetent, but an employer does not need this protection. He is the judge of the individual's worth and he often has the power of dismissal. . . . The maintenance of the ethical code which is often thought to be so important, hardly exists for these bodies. Where it does, it applies only to the small minority of independent practitioners, or is so vague as to be of no practical use. . . . the relationship between employer and employee has no need of such a code'.

In the passages quoted, Prandy[1] was writing principally about scientists and engineers but most of the points he makes could be applied to the planning profession.

Contracted Models of Professionalism

We can now begin to see a triangular model underlying much of the preceding discussion. The vertices represent: first, the organizational structure of planning agencies (especially local

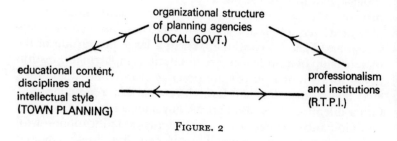

FIGURE. 2

government); secondly, skills, techniques and intellectual disciplines; thirdly, the nature and attitudes of professional institutions. The sides of the triangle represent the various kinds of interdependence between these three areas. Changes in plan-

[1] Kenneth Prandy, *Professional Employees*, Faber and Faber, London, 1965.

ning which we can foresee—in policy, analysis and design—impinge on each vertex. What we need to do here is to concentrate on the reactions occuring at the 'professionalism' vertex and to relate these in particular to the R.T.P.I.

It is clear that organizational structures are changing markedly. At the same time many different disciplines are being brought to bear on all the major aspects of planning. These changes look like being long-term and no one can forecast with any confidence (at least in detail) future organizational structure. In the nature of things no one can forecast in detail the mixes of skills and disciplines which will be needed in policy, analysis or design. If these two vertices (in our triangular model) must be flexible and adaptive to survive and grow in the face of uncertainty, the same must be true of professionalism.

Professions differ not only in the skills they represent but also in many other respects.[1] Sometimes these characteristics are related to the period during which the profession emerged, the nature of society at the time, the nature of its clients, the criteria of professional success or of malpractice, the degree of legal protection secured by the profession, its intellectual style and so on. For the sake of brevity, I have written below some of the most important dimensions for describing a profession. These are not mutually exclusive, and therefore the scheme is illustrative only. We should also remember that professions, like other institutions, are evolving all the time. How quickly, and along which dimensions, is the planning profession altering? Will the pattern and speed of change have to alter?

Generally old-established professions dominated by independent practitioners	*Generally new and emergent professions dominated by employment in public or private organizations and firms*
Single clients (mostly private)	Plural client groups
Severely restricted entry	Relatively free entry
Skill/technique dominated	Interest/attitude or problem dominated

---

[1] A. M. Carr-Saunders and P. A. Wilson, *The Professions*, (2nd edition, 1964), Cass, London, 1933.

Statutory regulation of practice	No statutory regulation of practice
Institutional sanctions over professional conduct	Job market sanctions over professional conduct
Clearly defined criteria of malpractice	No clearly definable criteria of malpractice
Apprenticeship training dominant	Academic education dominant
Educational content dominated by professional institution	Educational content determined academically
Little or no research tradition	Strong research tradition

A number of useful points can be made by reference to this diagram of the dimensions of professionalism. First, although it is difficult to think of examples which occupy extreme positions on all dimensions, some are fairly consistently at one or the other. Thus both solicitors and barristers are fairly close to the left-hand side on most dimensions, while computer professionals and social-welfare professionals are over at the right-hand side. Secondly, the left-hand side seems to reflect professions which grew up and became institutionalized in the eighteenth century but especially in the nineteenth century—surgery, engineering, accountancy—whereas right-hand positions are more characteristic of the present century. Thirdly, secular changes tend to move professions steadily towards the right along all the dimensions, albeit at differing speeds. Finally, there seems to be some kind of internal consistency in the scheme; for example, institutional sanctions, statutory registration and severe restrictions on entry are all sensible positions where there are clearly defined criteria of malpractice, particularly with regard to individual clients—we are glad that surgeons and anaesthetists fall into this group. Equally, if there are no meaningful criteria for malpractice nor clearly-defined client groups, it seems reasonable to expect relatively free entry to the profession and for the employment 'market' to sort practitioners out by education, experience and reputation.

The Royal Town Planning Institute

We can examine the R.T.P.I. in relation to the above scheme. It is difficult to call to mind many situations in which a professional planner would advise a single private client—whether an individual or a company. No doubt there are still large landowners or developers who might occasionally commission a planner in private practice, but these situations are rare. City councils more frequently do so but they are the elected representatives of a highly plural set of overlapping publics without single, clearly-defined objectives. Planners appearing at public inquiries or appeals about planning decisions do so in the rôle of expert witness where the key professional rôle is that of the lawyer and advocate. Undoubtedly, the planning profession is largely, and increasingly, in the public service of *plural client groups*, i.e. well towards the right-hand side of the scale.

Entry to the R.T.P.I. is fairly severely restricted. Corporate membership is limited to those who have passed the Institute's examinations or have been exempted by success in a 'recognized' educational course.[1] Attempts to widen the scope of entry to the Institute and to allow people to enter more freely have been the subject of heated debate in recent years.[2] Closely related to this question is that of the nature of planning in the technical sense—what is the 'core-skill', if any, or is planning a field of operation for several skills working in multi-disciplinary teams? This is a very complex issue indeed and opinions vary greatly, but the R.T.P.I.'s official attitude in the recent past seems to represent a move towards identification with a unique skill.

There is *no statutory regulation of practice* as a planner in the strict sense of registration of medical practitioners, or the legal control over the appellation 'architect'. Anyone may call himself a 'planner' or 'planning consultant', though the Royal Charter safeguards the appellation 'Chartered Town Planner'. But we must emphasize the very real effects on *entry to, and promotion within, the local government service* exerted by the need to be a corporate member of the R.T.P.I., and we repeat that so long as local government has separate planning departments headed by Chartered Planners this situation is likely to persist.

This close connection between the R.T.P.I. and planning in the local government service results in a dualism over sanctions on conduct. The R.T.P.I. exercise sanctions over its members

---

[1] Cockburn, *op. cit.* a.   [2] Cockburn, *op. cit.* c, Chapters 3, 4 and 5.

on issues typical of professional bodies (e.g. charging less than the minimum fee for a job), while local government exercises others (e.g. not allowing private practice or dealings in land within the authority's jurisdiction).

A surgeon's errors can be fatal, an engineer's disastrous, an accountant's very costly. Are there any similar criteria for malpractice on the part of a planner? Even if it were possible to define when a town or region had 'gone wrong', the state of affairs could be attributable to hundreds of very complex reasons, hardly any of which might be under the planners' control. And who would sue the planner? The city council who paid his fee? The Lord Mayor? The industrialists? The tradespeople? One of the cornerstones of professional institutions is the protection they offer (via sanctions) to their members' clients against malpractice and incompetence. But both 'client' and 'competence' must be capable of definition without any ambiguity; *neither of these conditions is met or ever could be met with respect to planning*.[1]

In keeping with similar trends in almost all professions, the education of planners has shifted from an apprenticeship system in which would-be entrants study part-time while 'sitting at the feet of the master' towards a system based very largely on full-time education in university or similar institutions; the process is virtually complete in the planning profession.

When apprenticeship is the rule, it is entirely consistent, indeed necessary, for the professional institute to run its own examinations and to keep a firm controlling hand over the apprentices' studies and experience. As this system is replaced by more and more full-time academic education, institutions typically relax their grip. For various reasons the R.T.P.I. retains its own examinations. It also has a very powerful influence on the content of courses in higher education which it 'recognizes' or which seek recognition (via the Visiting Board system). Considerable pressures are now being put on the R.T.P.I. to review, relax or even abandon this system, especially by bodies such as the recently-formed Education for Planning Association.

---

[1] F. A. R. Bennion, *Professional ethics: the consultant professions and their code*, Charles Knight, London, 1969.

At the same time, the research tradition, which has been almost completely absent in planning, is growing rapidly, especially since the establishment of the S.S.R.C. and the C.E.S. But much of the research, perhaps the greater part, is carried out in institutions which have no direct relationship with the R.T.P.I., either formally (*via* the recognized course system) or in terms of intellectual orientation. And although the R.T.P.I. itself has had a Research Committee for many years (latterly an 'Advisory Group') and has published four editions of a 'Register of Planning Research', it has yet to make any significant impact on the intellectual community.

We can now put the foregoing analysis down in graphical form:

Clients	Single □⟶	Plural
entry	restricted □⟶ ?	unrestricted
practical orientation	techniques □⟶	problems
regulation	statutory □	non-statutory
conduct standards	institutional □⟶?	job-market
criteria of competence	definable □⟶	undefinable
education method	apprenticeship □⟶	academic
education content	institutional □⟶ ?	academic
research tradition	weak □⟶	strong

FIGURE. 3

This illustrates some of the problems now facing the R.T.P.I. Like several other professions, planning is developing a research tradition, education in the wider sense is becoming more and more influenced by academic rather than 'craft' considerations, and its clients are less and less identifiable as individuals or corporate groups. The jobs planning must tackle over the next thirty years, and the political, social, economic and administrative environments in which these problems and their solutions will arise, are full of uncertainties. For the Institute itself, the key to the future would seem to lie partly within its own power to influence and the means would be membership and educational policy. But *the market for the employment of planners could exert a powerful influence on the Institute* and it is here that it is most vulnerable.

But planners—R.T.P.I.-type planners that is—have a number of strengths deriving from their background and from current trends concerning their rôle in government. We can once again look at these at two levels: first, the strategic or 'structural' policy level of work which will tend to be the dominant style of the upper tier in Britain and represented by the G.L.C., the metropolitan and non-metropolitan counties in England, the Welsh counties and the new Scottish 'regions'. Second, we can hazard some guesses about the particular strengths which planners might have at the local planning level which, together with personal and community services, will dominate the new district councils forming the second tier of local government in Britain and the closest direct links with the individuals, families and businesses served and affected by their actions.

At the district level, the work of local physical planning may become more closely related to the other community services—housing, primary education, personal and social welfare: the statutory device of the 'district' and 'action area' plans will require inter-service and inter-departmental co-operation, very often in task forces. This is especially true of remedial action in General Improvement Areas and Community Development projects. The ongoing work of development control could play an even bigger rôle than at present, in providing one part of the communication channels with the public and in providing colleagues throughout various departments with one of several 'windows on the world'.

It can be argued that development control work should become much more integrated horizontally with other agencies in the public service and with community groups; these links would usually be direct and face-to-face. At the same time there is a need to connect these realms of implementation and action much more richly with the policy and strategy realms in local government.

In this latter realm of policy design, of analysis, but especially in helping in the work of 'strategic choice', R.T.P.I.-type planners will have a big part to play—and conceivably some current advantage over other kinds of professionals. Because a large proportion of all major policies and decisions require the use of land and physical resources, and because spatial separation acts as a deterrent on accessibility and interaction, therefore town planners have opportunity and justification for being involved in strategic choice and policy work to a greater extent than most of their professional colleagues in government.

Already, of course, the clerks and the treasurers are integrators by necessity and via money-resource analysis respectively.

The town planners as we know them are thus well equipped by their 'comprehensive' ideology, by their knowledge and by their current rôles to act as integrators, as people who will help to build 'outward connectivity' from local government agencies as suggested by Friend and Yewlett,[1] and to act as the 'reticulists' (i.e. the people who build, maintain and operate along networks of communication) proposed by John Power.[2]

It is clear that the skills possessed by R.T.P.I. members may become more and more a matter of knowing how urban-regional governments work, how they can be reshaped and remoulded, how to 'play' these systems, how to foster or to obstruct change, what are the rules of this game and how the rules can be altered. As Friedson[3] puts it, professionals

> more and more formulate the rationale for the organizations and, particularly in the human services control the performance of the core of the work which is the prime justification for the existence of the organizations.

Conclusions

The planning profession and the R.T.P.I. carry the birthmarks of physical design and have evolved during half a century in which the principal consumers of its skills have been technique-orientated departments of local government. If problem-orientated, management-science methods come to the fore in the public services, the planning profession will be called upon to substantiate its asserted claim to a unique skill and contribution. If such claims cannot be substantiated then corporate membership of the Institute could carry far less weight in the employment market; conversely education, experience and reputation could count for more. Practice seems to be polarizing

---

[1] John K. Friend and C. J. L. Yewlett, *Inter-Agency decision processes: practice and prospect*, Tavistock Institute, London, 1971, I.O.R.

[2] John Power, *Planning: magic and technique*. I.O.R. Tavistock Institute, London, 1971.

[3] Eliot Friedson, Editorial Foreword to *American Behavioural Scientist*, Vol. 14, 1971, pp. 467-74.

towards (a) 'structure plan' levels where operational research, policy and management skills will predominate, (b) grass-roots 'local plan' levels where specific developmental and social-science skills will be needed. In both areas interdisciplinary work will be the rule and not the exception.

The continuing debates within the Town Planning Institute have centred around the education and membership policy, topics which are closely intertwined. These debates must have seemed to many interested onlookers to be often 'introverted and even narcissistic' and therefore 'it would be easy to overlook a third and potentially powerful interest group; central and local government, whose departments carry the statutory responsibility for planning in the widest sense.'

The institute has hitherto committed its future somewhat excessively on the question of techniques and the employment market. What it has done in the past, and what it hopes to continue doing, is to qualify people with a set of skills most of which are possessed by others, and which lack any distinct and united theoretical underpinning or value system. At the same time it hopes that its corporate members will enjoy what are virtually monopoly rights in a particular part of the employment market but, as we have seen, these markets are being 'reshaped beyond recognition'. Moreover, in the opinion of some people 'it is against the public interest that the unqualified should be barred from offering a service except where the service involves risk of a specially serious kind and degree to clients who are unable to assess the danger of using the services of unqualified practitioners, or to the interests of third parties'.[1]

Since this chapter was first drafted, the debate within the R.T.P.I. has taken yet another turn with the circulation to the membership in December 1971 of a 'discussion paper on membership policy'.[2] The authors of this note review the changes affecting the Institute directly (new techniques, the new legislation) and the development of related processes of planning and management (social, economic, corporate and community planning). They also draw attention to changes in the structure and functions of central and local government and

---

[1] Monopolies Commission, *op. cit.*, para. 310.
[2] Royal Town Planning Institute, *op. cit.*, 1971.

in the content and nature of educational programmes affecting planners, i.e. 'planning-related' courses.

They go on to discuss briefly the future rôle of the Institute and in particular they draw a distinction between professional and learned societies. No real comment is offered on the views that professionalism may be an outdated concept and that town planning is not really a unique skill but a context for the operation of many kinds of skills. The third point—that flexibility is needed to cope with the turbulence of change and uncertainty surrounding the Institute and that an inflexible body inhibits the necessary freedom of response—is, however, discussed briefly in relation to the suggestion of a 'learned society' rôle. The authors of the discussion note are very doubtful about this and the consequences of the absence of a town planning profession for society:

> There would be no body to develop the concept and practice of town planning, no official body to speak authoritatively about planning to the Government and the public, no recognized body to relate the town planning job to education in this field. Educational bodies would be free to develop their courses, but to what end? Yardsticks are inconvenient but their removal leaves a void. Even those most critical of this Institute would be unlikely to expect a unilateral dismantling of the profession; change in this field seems more likely to be related to change regarding all professions and ways in which society would substitute other forms of checks and balances. It is more relevant for the profession to consider ways in which it can adapt to change *as a profession, together with some adaptation of the professional rôle, rather than by drastic removal of the professional rôle* (p. 9, emphasis added).

In view of the authors of the note, then, (if not of the Institute) the R.T.P.I. *uniquely* develops the concepts and practice of town planning and can speak 'authoritatively' to the Government and the public. Despite the posture of the note, educators are busily innovating without reference to this 'recognized body' and are quite happy to debate and try to define their educational goals without the advice of the Institute. For them, the 'void' of the R.T.P.I.'s hypothetical disbandment as a qualifying association would seem to hold no terrors.

The remainder of the document, having virtually dismissed the learned society rôle (except as a cock-shy alternative) is

D

occupied by a discussion of what *professional* 'field of interest' the Institute should seek to represent—environmental planning (i.e. spatial and land-use), community planning (environmental plus social and economic planning) or corporate and community planning, i.e. focusing on the *process* of planning itself, embracing 'all planning/management activities exercised in the field of the environment, including perhaps educational, financial and other planning activities related to the corporate planning process' (p. 12). This very wide latter field of interest is used as the basis of the only *non*-professional option offered for discussion, i.e. the 'learned society' option without formal tests of competence like the other four major options.

It is not possible to give a full evaluation of the discussion note, since at the time of writing the R.T.P.I. members have not yet responded to it. Nevertheless, as it stands it shows how closely the Institute's awareness of the major dimensions of the problem accord with those we have set out above in this chapter. Although the change from a qualifying association to a learned society is admittedly 'drastic' we believe that the case against it is overstated by the note and that its advantages are not fully brought out. The central problems (e.g. such as possession of unique rare skills and well-defined criteria of malpractice) are nettles which the Institute's authors do not grasp.

Clearly the Town Planning Institute, like any professional qualifying association whose membership is largely in salaried employment, is in a precarious position if it relies heavily on its 'job-ticket' function for retaining the allegiance of members. But it seems clear that 'unless associations take more trouble to stimulate membership participation in meetings and publications, many organizations may decline even deeper into pure diploma-awarding bodies, the majority of members being solely interested in the designatory letters and unconcerned with corporate life'.[1]

The Institute could find itself in a precarious position if access to senior posts is made much less dependent on Institute membership (which seems at least probable). Its best strategy might be not only to widen but completely to alter the basis for its membership. Rather than being closed to all save those

---

[1] Millerson, *op. cit.*, p. 218.

possessing certain examinable skills it should be open to all showing evidence of a similar point of view or way of thinking. One part of this common focus would be an understanding of how towns and regions 'work' in general, and some specialized knowledge of one or more (spatial or functional) subsystems, problems and techniques. One of its major functions in the future could be to act as an acknowledged centre for fostering and advancing the *understanding* of cities, regions and their governance—especially the spatial and place-related aspects of society and its problems. It should replace its primary concern of qualifications and employment with dominant interests in *learning* and in *values*.

The values which would be relevant to the ethical concerns of a new-style planning profession would reflect the governmental context we have already discussed, the social milieu of the operations of planning authorities' policies—sometimes as 'clients' or client-groups, sometimes as the subject of studies in order to formulate, test and modify policies and their mode of implementation.

The 'morality' of a planning professional would, therefore, be in part the morality of any good public official—a concern for civic rights, personal freedom, the right to information and to privacy, a concern for the effectiveness but also the accountability of government. Also it would in part be a morality of any humane and perceptive person, e.g. refusing to exploit individuals as 'case studies' or examples and refusing to over-dramatize events or their interpretation. Similarly, as would fit a 'learned society' or 'study association' image, there would be the familiar scholarly respect for accuracy, logic and clarity, for cautious interpretation of evidence, but a willingness to produce clear conclusions where this can be done, neither 'pussy-footing' nor giving deliberate offence.[1]

The attainment of such standards of behaviour and such attitudes do not require a qualifying institution as defined and discussed in the literature. Academic traditions of scholarship and the public-service traditions of conduct are evolving and changing in detail but really not in broad principle. In combination they would do all that a qualifying body could claim

---

[1] F. A. R. Bennion, *op. cit.*, 1969.

to do (except where expulsion meant loss of the right to practice, as in the case of doctors and the B.M.A.).

In a very real sense, the problems of towns and regions are the problems of human society and its governmental agencies, national, regional and local. The 'definite service' which the profession and its Institute could provide in the coming years will clearly not be any precisely-defined technical operation. Rather it should encompass a growing body of theoretical understanding and empirical knowledge about urban-regional systems and governments, and the essentially political values they embody. Now a sense of value is not easily taught or examined or discernible in a record of a candidate's early practical experience. But the values we are talking about here are fundamental rather than instrumental, since the candidate would not be seeking corporate membership as a kind of union card but rather looking towards the Institute as an intellectual and spiritual home—which was probably uppermost in the minds of those who sat down to dinner in November 1913 to propose its foundation.

Chapter Six

Planning and Government

DAVID DONNISON

Introduction

I begin this chapter by explaining why planners should be concerned about the administrative and political systems within which they work. Next I note some of the social changes which are likely to affect these systems during the coming years. Then comes the central section of the chapter: a brief discussion of various levels of government in which planners have a part to play. As in previous chapters, the discussion deals with the period to the end of the twentieth century. Although a number of contemporary debates are mentioned—and their importance probably over-emphasized—our main purpose is not to contribute to these debates but to speculate about developments which may affect planning and planners over a longer time span. I conclude with a few more general comments about planning and its relationship to government.

The Government of Planning

Since it is centrally concerned with the allocation of resources and access to opportunities, planning is a political process: government—its legal powers, administrative structure and political culture—forms the mould in which it is cast. Thus planners must be alert to the constraints imposed on their work and thinking by the constitutions within which they operate, and be prepared to seek changes in these systems of government when necessary. Their professional training should, in part, be an education in political science and social administration. Government itself is plannable.

In Britain the strongest institutions of government operate either on a national scale or on the scale of the county and county borough. When local government took its present shape during the last quarter of the nineteenth century, no one was thinking of the planning tasks that were to be conferred on it in 1947. By then local authorities were in many ways inappropriate for the job. Yet many of our planning concepts, powers and procedures have evolved as a response to the problems which the planning authorities have to cope with. And many of the reforms now being discussed are attempts to tackle the regional and neighbourhood problems that arise at scales larger or smaller than that of the county or county borough. Planning is culture-bound, as a glance at other countries shows.

In France, where central government has greater power and prestige and spends a larger proportion of the national income than the governments of most market economies, planning law gives the public few formal opportunities to object to proposals for development, planners are less dependent than their British colleagues on municipal planning committees and spend less time at public inquiries and on the preparation of decisions formulated to withstand criticism at such inquiries.

In the United States much of the work that would in Britain be left to the discretion of planners is conducted by passing zoning laws which prescribe uses and densities for land. When such laws have been enacted, they may be effectively interpreted by lawyers arguing on behalf of their clients and by part-time planning commissions. Thus people who want to secure decisions about urban development that will help particular groups naturally turn to 'advocacy planning', seeking the most cogent legal spokesmen for their chosen clients. In other countries advocacy planning is a less natural and often a less effective way of getting things done.

Every country could furnish further illustrations of the culture-bound character of planning; and it is government which furnishes the most important parts of the culture. In Britain the public services are now undergoing the most extensive re-organization they have experienced in two generations. Major reforms are under way in the Civil Service, a Royal Commission is examining the British constitution and the case for new forms of provincial government, and the entire structure of local government and its finances are to be recast. The health services are likely to be given a completely new administrative structure, and the personal social services and the law courts are being completely re-organized. It is too early to guess at the outcome of these reforms; even when the necessary legislation is complete it will take years for new patterns to evolve. But if town planners do not play a constructive part in shaping these patterns, they will find once again that their work has been fitted into a system derived from other traditions and designed for other purposes—which would be ironical, when so many agree that

> in no field is the present shape of local government less well adapted to current needs than in planning; and indeed it was the planning interest which, more than any other, forced the new look at the organization of local government.[1]

Some Changes

I shall not try to summarize all the influences which are helping to shape this country's systems of government. Many of them were considered in our previous book. But some of the most important of them must be briefly noted before we turn to the main topics of this chapter.

In the longer run it will be the intellectual developments that exert most influence. We are beginning (although only beginning) to understand how cities and regions 'work'—how the pace and pattern of economic and social development are determined, and how the opportunities offered by an urban, industrial society are distributed. Everything depends on everything else. Thus to bring about one change we may have to change a lot of other things, and any major change is liable to produce unforeseen repercussions. 'Planning', as conceived under the 1947 Act, dealt particularly with land-uses and the arrangement and appearance of buildings and other physical objects. The counties and county boroughs on which these powers were conferred had a scale and shape that made any other interpretation of planning difficult. Growing concern

---

[1] Evelyn Sharp, *The Ministry of Housing and Local Government*, Allen and Unwin, 1969, p. 139.

about the country's economic structure and growth and about
major urban rebuilding schemes drew town planners into
social and economic planning on bigger and on smaller geographical scales than those they had been accustomed to. Since
labour markets, overspill schemes and commuting, shopping
and recreational patterns extended well beyond the boundaries
of the planning authorities, attempts to plan their development
took shape in new planning councils, consortia and study groups
covering larger areas. More recently town planners have recognized that their work should form an integral part of programmes for the attainment of broader social objectives through
the co-ordinated management of all services operating at the
level of government in question. Once again, new approaches
have been made possible by new patterns of organization, often
beginning—as Brian McLoughlin has pointed out[1]—in new
authorities, ranging in size from Crawley to the Greater London
Council, which seized opportunities for innovation when the
mould of earlier patterns of organization was broken.

But despite changing fashions of debate and some real changes
in practice, much the same people have in most authorities had
to go on doing much the same work as before. Although they
may talk about 'corporate planning', development control and
other old-fashioned tasks continue because the public expect,
and the law obliges, local authorities to perform them. But it is
growing clearer that these old-fashioned tasks are part of a
more extensive pattern of activities which should be more
effectively linked to each other. These activities can be distinguished by the types of 'output' expected from them. All of
them are important, and there is no hierarchical significance
about the order in which the following list is presented:

1. *Designing* and redesigning parts of the built environment,
   ranging in scale from a pedestrian crossing to a new town.
   Planners doing this work are providing a specialized, professional service. In the larger projects, the planning team
   will have to include many disciplines and professions.

2. *Controlling development.* Under this heading town planners
   regulate the activities of other designers and investors, in
   private and public sectors of the market.

---

[1] *A Future for Development Control*, April 1971; unpublished paper.

3. *Structure planning* deals with 'the social, economic and physical system of an area, so far as they are subject to planning control or influence', including 'the distribution of the population, the activities and the relationships between them, the patterns of land-use and the development the activities give rise to, together with the network of communications and the systems of utility services'.[1] To do this work well, planners must be alert to its implications for the economic and social development of the whole surrounding region, and they must recruit an array of disciplines competent for that task. But they are not themselves planning the whole economic and social development of the region: they are doing the job required of them by the Town and Country Planning Acts.

4. *Policy planning*, based on no specific Act of Parliament but dealing with the general development of the whole area and the contribution to be made to that development by all the public services of the authority concerned.[2] This work, sometimes called 'corporate' or 'comprehensive' planning, calls for forecasts of revenue and expenditure, the determination of general priorities and policies, and the monitoring of their outcomes. It must serve the political leaders or top management of the organization concerned, and draw on the help of all its departments. No profession or department has any presumptive right to direct this work.

'Strategic planning' links structure planning to policy planning and provides a context for each of them, but the phrase has been used in so many ways—some merely rhetorical—that its meaning is difficult to define precisely.

The development and differentiation of these kinds of work has been carried forward by new data, analysed in new ways with the help of computers. The need for closer links between these forms of planning is gradually being recognized. What begins on the design-planner's drawing board as, say, a shopping precinct, calls for decisions from those responsible for

---

[1] *Development Plans. A Manual on Form and Content*, H.M.S.O., 1970, p. 18.
[2] See J. D. Stewart. 'Corporate Planning and Structure Planning', *Local Government Finance*, Vol. 75, No. 5, 1971; p. 130, for a useful discussion of these activities and the relationships between them.

development control, makes its impact upon the distribution of activities and the flows of traffic within the county's structure plan, and creates opportunities and repercussions for several other public services which figure in the authority's broader policy plans. Meanwhile many public services should feed back information to guide town planners in their work—some of which will make further demands on other services. A rise in the number of homeless people whose children have to be cared for by the social services department, for example, may call for top level policy decisions allocating more land for public housing, a more determined strategy for the retention of existing rented houses, and greater efforts from the housing department to get rent allowances to poorer families. To co-ordinate these different kinds of planning in each department of government, the same information must be made promptly available to all, but in different 'languages' to meet their different needs.

This information and the skills required to handle it are expensive. To conduct and co-ordinate the different kinds of planning they will have to do, local authorities will have to invest in training and equipment on a larger scale than hitherto; and new kinds of staff, qualified for research and intelligence work, will have to play a larger part in their affairs.

Until recently town planners led a relatively sheltered life. Ordinary people seldom paid much attention to them unless brought into contact with development control by the need to secure permission for the building of a garage or a bow window —and these were scarcely occasions for political uproar. Educational administrators closing grammar schools and housing managers putting up council rents often had a much stormier time. Now this is changing. The hornets' nests stirred up by motorway and airport proposals are forerunners of a new climate of opinion in which planners will have to cope with a public that is better informed, more demanding and more aggressively organized. People are growing more alert to their rights, more sophisticated politically, and less deferential towards officials.

The recent growth of amenity societies, action groups and associations representing the users of health services, state education and social security benefits shows that all the public services face a more demanding public. But this development may go further in the town planning field—partly because of rising public concern about noise, pollution, congestion and other problems lumped together as 'environmental', but mainly because the next thirty years will see the complete renewal or rebuilding of the inner parts of our older towns, and the creation of new urban communications systems and central areas. Until the 1960s investment had usually been concentrated on development at the fringes of major centres, and private and public developers alike dealt with planners on behalf of a distant and generally uncomprehending public. When they are being planned, no one knows who the residents of a new estate or the pupils of a new school will be. But ordinary people are far more directly affected by redevelopment which cuts deeply into long established residential areas, destroys familiar landmarks and services, brings newcomers into the district, creates new traffic channels and destroys old ones. They know more, care more, and are more likely to make demands on the planners held to be responsible for these changes.

The proliferation of regional planning boards and advisory councils, joint planning committees and regional planning teams, and their survival under successive governments, shows that a sustained attempt is being made to plan more comprehensively on a regional scale. Regional planning is here to stay—in the sense both of 'national regional' plans dealing mainly with the allocation of major economic resources, and of 'regional local' plans dealing with the location of physical investment within regions.[1]

Meanwhile another series of developments shows that this country is also searching for means to focus attention and resources on areas much smaller than the present planning authorities. The town planners' action areas, educational priority areas, community development projects, the area social service teams proposed by the Seebohm Committee, the Skeffington Committee's community fora, the voluntary community action groups and advisory centres, and proposals for a nationwide system of elected neighbourhood councils—all these are partly a recognition of the need for more effective

---

[1] The terms are Peter Hall's—helpfully explained and contrasted in *Theory and Practice of Regional Planning*, Pemberton Books, 1970.

government at a geographical scale much smaller than the county or county borough. There has also been a boom in the work and spending of rural parishes. These movements are likely to grow stronger and more purposeful as people now engaged on sporadic, independent neighbourhood projects recognize their common interests. They will gain further support as the reform of local government produces even larger local authorities, felt to be more remote than those we now have.

These are some of the main developments which are compelling us to re-appraise and reform the governmental systems in which various kinds of 'planning' are done. The structure of the urban economy is changing and we are beginning to understand it better. New ideas about decision-making are entering government, together with a lot more information that may help decision-makers and will certainly complicate their task. As planners assume more explicit responsibilities for development and redevelopment, they must do business with a public that makes more insistent and more contradictory demands. In many different quarters people are trying to devise better procedures for coping with problems that arise at geographical scales larger and smaller than that of the present local planning authorities. Town planners should play their part in shaping the outcome of these pressures. Otherwise their own contribution to society may again be constrained by an administrative and political framework which neither poses the problems they should be considering nor gives anyone the powers to resolve them.

So large a topic deserves a book to itself. In these few pages I shall only comment on a few of the points that book might deal with, taking each level of government in turn from the largest to the smallest.

International Agencies

A growing number of the problems which planners deal with call for action on an international scale. Rising concern about pollution of air and water has brought home to everyone the limitations of planning that stops at national frontiers. But strategic planning of a country's economic and social development and corporate policy planning must both involve many departments of government and many professions. Each may need its own links with other countries, but a single, international planning agency with general responsibilities—a planners' equivalent to the World Health Organization—is unlikely to be effective. More specific tasks, such as the rebuilding of cities devastated by earthquakes or the co-ordination of plans for frontier regions, can be tackled by international planning teams. But a team that manages the continuing development of a city or region has to be more deeply rooted in the power structure of the society concerned than an international group can normally be.

Specialized international agencies will play an increasingly important part in interchanging ideas and information. Interchange is certainly needed: planners in this country still rely mainly on the literature available in English, and hence on research in Britain and the United States. The library of a local planning department cannot yet supply so richly international a literature as can be available to departments concerned with public health or education. That is the fault of research workers rather than practising planners, and international centres for research in this field have been set up to remedy the deficiency. But the main responsibilities will continue to rest with universities and other national centres of learning. If their work is good enough, they soon form links which give them an international rôle. If it is not, international institutes and research centres are unlikely to do better.

Central Government

At the level of our own central government, a massive merger has just occurred in the Department of the Environment. A giant department will achieve nothing by itself: the ministers and permanent secretaries of its previously separate parts were already too busy. It is too early to say what opportunities the merger will afford for new and more creative division of the work to be done, but some pointers to the future can be discerned. Main responsibility for national economic strategies, and hence for the major allocations of investment and population between regions, is likely to remain with the 'economic' departments of central government. Main responsibility for the allocation of resources and people within regions is likely to fall increasingly to the Department of the Environment. That

department has also become the central government's spokes-
man for the 'quality of the environment'; this role, which is
likely to be a permanent one, cannot be assumed by departments mainly responsible for production, trade and consumption. The frightening size of the new department means that
the devolution and decentralization of responsibilities to lower
levels of government, so long preached at the Ministry of
Housing and Local Government, is now more urgently needed
than ever.

What part will The Central Policy Review Staff play? To
judge from past experience—extending back to Lloyd George's
kindergarten—central units for the review of national policies
are likely to be a recurring rather than a permanent feature
of the scene. There are good reasons for their mutability. Each
administration has to find its own way of breaking the cast of
mind established by its predecessors. To pose old questions
afresh and to focus the attention of government upon a few,
simplified, new-minted priorities, each administration must
recruit people—usually from business or the academic world—
who have no spiritual capital invested in past programmes and
not too many anxieties about the future.

Regional Government

The scope for shifting responsibilities for day-to-day administration out of the central departments will depend partly on
the strength of regional government. I shall use the word
'region' to refer to a province roughly equivalent in scale to the
United Kingdom's eleven economic planning regions, which are
themselves of widely varying size and wealth.

Regional administrative and consultative bodies of various
kinds—for health, water, tourism, planning of all sorts, and
many other purposes—are likely to grow stronger: there are so
many problems that cannot be effectively handled by the
present local authorities or the larger ones we are to have in
future.

The creation of the provincial governments which Derek
Senior has called for[1] would demand a transfer of powers to

---

[1] Report of the Royal Commission on Local Government in England,
1966–1969, Vol. II, *Memorandum of Dissent*, Cmnd. 4040.

multi-purpose bodies, with authority to redeploy resources and sufficient political strength to implement decisions against serious opposition. And that is an altogether different matter. Provincial administrations inevitably compete with each other for national resources. Thus it is easier to generate a continuing and constructive provincial politics in deprived regions which normally stand to gain from the redistribution of national resources. (Easier, but not easy: how many regional politicians can you name?) That is why Scotland, Wales and the North-East have proved somewhat more effective political units than the West Midlands or the South-East. A body of politicians frankly devoted to securing more resources for the West Midlands at the expense of poorer regions would not be given much power by central government; a body devoted to restraining growth in that province for the sake of others poorer than themselves is unlikely to recruit a talented and enthusiastic band of politicians—or to get re-elected.

The present regional offices only secure staff sufficiently numerous and independent to stand up to Whitehall if they have the political support of a provincial patriotism. I have made no scientific study of these groups, but the typical official in Stormont or St. Andrew's House appears to have no exaggerated respect for the judgement of his colleagues in Whitehall, and is seldom eager to move his family to the London suburbs. Similar attitudes are to be found in Cardiff. Meanwhile, although the typical official in the smaller team to be found in the North-West Region is probably finding Manchester a nicer place than he had expected, he often defends his departmental superiors' policies with all the greater obstinacy for being less closely informed about them than he used to be when he worked in London, and he is reluctant to do anything that would long delay a return to the Home Counties.

Britain, we must remember, is about the size of California and produces about the same income for a population about twice as large. Outside the island's Celtic fringes—and often there, too—we are likely to find that the main questions which cannot be resolved by a strengthened system of local government are national in character. The building of a motorway or a university, or the closure of a shipyard or pit, each call for decisions that will in any case be made by ministers. Those representing the major interests involved—bodies such as the

N.U.M., Vickers and the U.G.C.—all have their head offices in London and are all capable of getting an interview with the minister any time they are aggrieved by such decisions, no matter how imposing a layer of provincial government is interpolated below him.

Thus something more genuinely resembling a provincial government may develop in Scotland and Wales but if similar institutions are set up in England they are unlikely to gain much independent power. Moreover, if we believe that every government should have an effective opposition with a real chance of gaining office, we must in any case be cautious about devolving powers to provincial administrations, for opposition is often deplorably weak at that level.

Local Government

We have been tempted to add to the already voluminous literature about the reform of local government, but the die will have been cast by the time this book appears, so we have resolved instead to consider the longer-term opportunities that reform may offer. Any re-organization sufficiently extensive to bring in a lot of new councillors and senior officials is apt to provoke further developments which may prove more important than the initial reform. Something like that happened in London after 1964.

Since every local authority has different strengths and weaknesses, and faces different problems, no single prescription can meet the needs of all of them. Dogmatic though they may appear, the proposals that follow are intended only to formulate some of the needs and tendencies to which planners should be alert during the coming years.

Major local authorities will need an effective policy planning unit which advises the council and its central policy committee about needs, priorities and strategies for the development of the area and its services. This unit would rely for much of its information on the 'line' departments responsible for these services—including education, personal social services and passenger transport, for example—and would help them with their own planning. The staff for this work should probably be drawn from most of the line departments, and would often return to them later in their careers: policy planning cannot be the preserve of any single profession. For the reasons already given when discussing the central government's policy review units, the form and membership of such groups are likely to change from time to time; but some group capable of doing this job will be permanently needed. Closely related to the policy planning unit must be the finance department, and a development department. The latter would be responsible for structure planning, major design planning and general policies for development control. Whether the three groups, concerned respectively with general priorities, finance and development, ought to be organized as one, two or three departments should depend on the needs, resources and personalities of the authority concerned.

Routine development control is henceforth to be conducted by the lower tier of district authorities, where it will often be constructive to place a good deal of smaller-scale design planning too. Development control should be a window on the world for all the other types of planner listed on pages 96 and 97. It shows the growth of new demands (more hotels, school car parks, student hostels and Sikh temples, for example) and the decline of old ones (fewer company football clubs, cinemas, cycle repair shops and landladies' lodgings). Other local services play a similar rôle: the personal social services may be among the first to spot a growth in the numbers of immigrant families, the schools should learn sooner than most about changes in the labour market for teenagers, and the housing department's responsibilities for rent allowances may prove to be a sensitive barometer of poverty. To ensure that all this information is analysed and interpreted in ways that structure and policy planners can use, and to get it fed back to 'line' departments which should take action upon it, the authority will need a strong central intelligence unit serving all branches of the organization.

Housing plays so important a part in determining urban structure and land-uses, the movement of people and the opportunities they secure, that it calls for special comment. This country has made no general re-appraisal of its housing needs and policies since the Royal Commission on the Housing of the Working Classes reported in 1885. (Housing has had no equivalent to Beveridge, Maud, Seebohm or the successive reports of the Central Advisory Councils for Education.)

Powers to intervene in the housing market have accumulated over the years in response to successive crises, pressures and fashions. Local authorities can build, acquire and demolish houses; they can set up housing advisory services, help people to move to new and expanding towns, and provide temporary shelter for homeless people; they can make improvement grants, lend money and offer professional advice to house buyers and housing associations; they can close houses, compel private owners to improve them, or impose management and control orders on them—and much else besides. But most of these powers are administered not by housing departments but by health, treasurers', clerks', social service and every other department imaginable. As a result, many of them are not treated as an instrument of housing policy at all. Neither are they used purposefully to extend people's mobility or to enlarge their opportunities. (Loans for house purchase and discretionary improvement grants, for example, may go not to those whom the authority wishes to recruit or to retain in its area, or to people who find it difficult to secure credit in the open market, but merely to those whom the treasurers' or clerks' departments regard as the best risks.) The new Housing Finance Act should provide an opportunity for bringing most of these powers together into one department under one director of housing services, responsible not merely for administering council housing but for helping people satisfy their own housing needs in any way that seems best to them—for example, by buying or improving a home, by moving to places where housing is cheaper or jobs more plentiful, or by getting their rent fixed by the rent officer.

In the metropolitan areas we shall need a division of housing powers between the upper and lower tiers, roughly equivalent to the arrangements to be adopted for planning. Some of the district authorities will need the resources and leadership of a larger authority which exercises, like the Greater London Council, a more general responsibility for the housing of the whole metropolis.

Neighbourhoods

Finally I turn to the lowest level in the hierarchy of public authorities: the neighbourhood or parish. As I noted on pages

99 and 100, this level has been attracting growing interest in many quarters. But the sizes of the neighbourhoods people are talking about vary a great deal: the Seebohm Report recommended area teams serving populations of 50 000 to 100 000. Advocates of a nationwide system of neighbourhood councils have said they should typically serve populations of 5000 to 10 000. Educational priority areas or the planners' action areas might be smaller still—or much larger.

The motives of those proposing such schemes vary as widely. Most fall into one or more of three broad categories:

1. *Redistribution.* Attempts to focus outside attention or to generate indigenous pressures which will secure more resources for deprived areas in order to improve their living conditions, public services and attainments—for example through educational priority areas and community development projects.

2. *Effectiveness.* Attempts to manage public services more effectively by exposing officials to local demands, giving them a more comprehensive and comprehensible task, and securing better co-ordinated action between different services at ground level—for example, through planning action areas and Seebohm area teams.

3. *Participation.* Attempts to enable people to participate in their own government through local groups capable of formulating their own demands, setting up their own services and doing things for themselves which otherwise would not get done—for example, through parishes and neighbourhood councils.

These aims can often be reconciled. Community development projects, for example, are intended to secure resources for deprived areas, to make public services more responsive to local needs, and to help residents to voice their demands and run projects of their own. But sometimes there will be conflicts. Neighbourhood councils, if we had a nationwide network of them, would probably promote more participation in the richer areas where people are accustomed to this style of social action; if so, that would conflict with a policy of redistribution in favour of poorer areas. Where these aims conflict, a choice of priorities must be made. My own would generally take the order shown above: Derek Senior, in the next chapter, proposes rather different priorities.

But advance in any of these directions will have to surmount formidable opposition. Arrayed against the co-ordinating intentions of some advocates of neighbourhood service centres are the traditions of a highly departmentalized local government, sustained by the departmentalism of central government and the *esprit de corps* of public service professions. Arrayed against any independent public participation in government are local politicians, always wary of any participation which is not channelled directly through themselves. Redistributive policies conflict with the tradition that *equal* shares (equal expenditure per rate-payer, per pupil, client or patient) are 'fair' shares.[1]

Some planners, aware of these obstacles but determined to concentrate and co-ordinate resources more effectively on the renewal of inner urban areas, have revived earlier proposals for the creation of 'old town' development corporations, to be appointed by central government for this work. The Milner Holland Committee hinted at something similar.[2] However, that proposal, if it was ever seaworthy, has been stranded by the tide of events. Current efforts to fashion more comprehensive forms of economic and social planning, to devolve more responsibilities from Whitehall to local government, and to create a more accountable style of administration in which the public can participate more actively, make this an implausible moment for turning *ad hoc* development corporations loose in the inner urban china shop.

But to ridicule such proposals is not good enough. The problems to which they have been addressed are real. To make progress in dealing with them will call for a combination of three things: a sufficiently strong team of professional staff, drawn from different services and given some freedom of manoeuvre in serving a particular district; accredited and accountable local representatives capable of speaking for this team and their district in the town hall; and independent, voluntary action, by, and on behalf of, people living in the district. Each of these things has already been tried separately,

---

[1] This tradition is critically examined in the Plowden Report, *Children and their Primary Schools*, H.M.S.O., 1967, para. 148.

[2] Cmnd. 2605, 1965, pp. 122–3.

in community development projects, voluntary action groups and area offices, of various kinds. They need to be combined. The case for such a development and the problems it poses have been discussed elsewhere.[1] Here I offer no more than a brief illustration of the way in which a project of this sort might work, and how town planners might fit into it.

In deprived areas chosen for special attention, local authorities might set up neighbourhood services centres combining the functions of a citizens' advice bureau, and the local offices of the housing, social service, education, planning and other departments. To muster a team of this size, the centre would probably have to serve at least 25 000 people. Included in it there might be a public library, a planning office doing much of the planning department's design work for the area, and a housing aid service. Other services not provided by the local authority such as the community relations officer, the rent officer and some of the maternity and child welfare services (soon to be hived off to an area health authority?) might also be added. All the staff would be on the regular payroll of the normal statutory authorities, and their powers would be delegated from the town hall. They should be more readily available to the public and more alert to respond to local needs and aspirations than is sometimes possible in the town hall. Considerable responsibility for managing and developing these services should be delegated to the officers in charge of each, under the leadership of an area officer who would be generally responsible for all local authority services in his district. Most important of all, a richer and more concentrated mix of staff and expenditure would be brought to bear on the selected areas than elsewhere.

An area team of this sort must have properly accredited political spokesmen to speak for them and the area they serve. At the moment, chairmanship of party groups and policy committees, and of local government committees responsible for education, housing and other major spending services, give elected members more power than any other local post to which they can aspire. These are the routes to O.B.E.s and a

---

[1] David Donnison, 'The Micropolitics of The Inner City', in *London Urban Patterns, Problems and Policies* (to be published by Heinemann Educational Books, 1973).

seat on the bench. There is no local government committee for the Isle of Dogs, Liverpool 8, or Sparkbrook. In future there should be committees of elected members responsible for the combined local services of selected priority areas: the local councillors and aldermen, with co-opted members such as the local M.P., might together act as the management committee for such a local service centre. The politicians might hold their own meetings and 'surgeries' there. Without accredited political support of this kind, the project would wither.

The third element in this constitution for priority areas would be the groups representing the local community, ranging from the politically militant, through tenants' associations, to clubs and societies of less demanding kinds. Meeting rooms should be available at the local service centre for them. People from the area inquiring at the town hall about rents, rehousing, foster care and other matters would be advised to seek help from the local centre first. Thus it should become a local town hall: a source of services and advice, a focal point for pressures and complaints, and a forum for community action.

This proposal, for brevity's sake so dogmatically presented, is only an illustration of the kind of development that may be in the making. Many other versions could be envisaged. Their primary purposes would be to get more help to deprived areas in a form more responsive to local needs and more likely to stimulate local enterprise. To achieve that, such centres must be part of local government and draw on the full array of services available in the town hall; and they must be set up only in a few places, chosen for their special needs.

For planners seeking a clearer understanding of local aspirations, needs and resources in deprived 'action areas', closer collaboration with colleagues in other services, and a means of gaining public participation in planning and redevelopment on a scale of time and space that can be meaningful to ordinary people, such centres could offer an excellent base from which to work.

A development of this kind would breach all sorts of political and administrative conventions. Thus it would not get far without some initiative and financial support from central government. Room could be found for that in the government's urban programme.

Such centres should be distinguished from the neighbourhood

councils, outlined by Derek Senior in the next chapter. Since they are intended to encourage widespread participation in public affairs, neighbourhood councils should serve much smaller areas (there might be five or more to one of the service centres described here), they should presumably be set up everywhere, each should be directly elected and should appoint its own small staff. Although the two proposals have different aims they are not mutually exclusive: indeed, each might usefully complement the other.

Conclusion

There was a time when town planners felt obliged to justify their existence in face of criticism from those who regarded planning of all kinds as an unwarranted intrusion upon the market. It is now recognized that, although bad planning may indeed be more destructive than none at all, the option of a wholly unplanned society is no longer open. Plans of various kinds have to be made: if not by government, then by industrialists and developers (who cannot invest millions without some assurance that people will behave in ways that provide a return on their capital) and if not by town planners, then by those who must provide power and water supplies, transport systems, sewers and telephones. Moreover the planning processes which determine, in effect, what kind of neighbours we shall have, what it will cost to provide social services for them, and whether the outcome will enhance or blight our environment, are much too important to be cast aside. They are not idiosyncrasies we can adopt or abandon (like British summer time or early closing day), they are inventions which someone, somewhere, will use to his own advantage. Thus the question is not whether to plan, but who should plan, for what purposes, and to whom he should be accountable. Meanwhile if planning is 'here to stay', so are the forces of the market—even in centrally planned economies, as East European governments are recognizing. Economic, social and land-use planning cannot long proceed independently of each other: they must be part of the same strategy.

I have argued in this chapter that the central and local authorities will remain our principal instruments for planning. Provincial or regional bodies will play an important part in the process, but generally as a forum for the resolution of the conflicting needs of various central and local interests. Only in Scotland, Wales and Northern Ireland are more independent provincial authorities likely to emerge—and their independence will probably remain very limited. At the micro-political level of the urban neighbourhood or district, new forms of organization are taking shape in which town planners should play an active part. It is at this level that the ordinary citizen is likely to participate most vigorously in debate about planning.

The purpose of making government more accountable is to make it a more effective instrument for getting things done. In the United States the Right and the Left sometimes appear to collude in trying to make government powerless. Governments in Europe are more often treated as fallible but usable institutions and accorded a limited sovereignty—a tradition worth preserving and building on.

Positive planning policies will call for a formidable range of data and skills. Without more rigorous and economical techniques of analysis it will be impossible to cope with them—planning in the computer age would founder beneath the weight of its own uncomprehended print-outs. But analytical techniques and the systems theories from which they are derived will not by themselves produce a single plan. To furnish the options to be modelled and the criteria for testing them, we shall need fairly concrete and widely comprehended visions of the society we intend to create: something to replace the visions—now partly discredited but in their day enormously influential—of new towns, green belts and socially mixed neighbourhoods which inspired those who created our planning system.

Chapter Seven

Planning and the Public

DEREK SENIOR

To try to look ten, twenty, thirty years ahead in the field which forms the subject of this chapter is to be confirmed in the Johnsonian view of prophecy as the most gratuitous form of folly. No doubt some drastic changes must result from the present discontents among consumers of the output of the planning process, but any prediction as to what form such changes will take must be so precariously based on a pyramid of debatable assumptions about the future of every other aspect of planning that it can serve no useful purpose.

In the light of the Cublington and Aklam Road revolts, we might take as a generally acceptable starting-point Donnison's forecast of 'a new climate of opinion, in which planners will have to cope with a public that is better informed, more demanding and more aggressively organized'. (Chapter Six, page 98). We might even, for the sake of argument, follow him in his resolve to face the danger that our opportunities will continue in the longer term to be straitjacketed by the only 'reform' of local government that can have been enacted by the time this book appears (*ibid.*). Beyond that, however, any attempt to foresee how the involvement of the public in the planning process is likely to develop must depend on a series of increasingly hazardous speculations. Nevertheless, the exercise may be worth while—not for the value of any long-term conclusions it may suggest, but for the light it may throw on more immediate issues. The exploration of such a complex of interdependent possibilities cannot help us to know where we shall get to; but at least it may help to clarify our thinking about where we should seek to go from here.

First we must consider what exactly we mean by 'planning', and what in this context we mean by 'the public'. By 'planning', do we mean only what the planning departments of our national and local authorities are at any given time required by statute to do? Or what they are actually doing? Or what they should be doing? Or what they cannot do but what should be done by regional planning authorities yet to be created? Or do we include the planning activities of other local government departments, of each local authority as a whole, of *ad hoc* public authorities, of private enterprise and of various co-operative associations among these and other agencies? And by 'the public', do we mean the people whose property rights as owners, tenants and/or would-be developers are directly affected by official planning proposals or development control decisions, or do we include 'third parties' whose interests, proprietorial and other, are also affected, or the community at large as having a collective interest in the impact of any kind of planning activity on its total environment?

As Peter Hall has indicated, the scope and the ideology of planning have developed enormously over the last dozen years, and especially over the last five years (Chapter Four, page 44). But several important distinctions have to be drawn when we come to consider this development in the context of the present chapter. In the first place, what planning means in practice will continue to be conditioned by both the structure of local government and the provisions of our planning legislation. As recently as July 1970 it was possible for the Rural District Councils Association to assert that

> The purpose of town and country planning is to control land use by the preparation of development plans (now structure plans and local plans), by the determination of individual applications for planning permission (within plan policy), by the eradication of unauthorized or non-conforming development and by the protection/preservation of amenity.[1]

It could as truly be asserted that the purpose of the National Health Service is to control the spread of cholera; but if, for the rest of this century, development control outside the

---

[1] Rural District Councils Association: The New District Councils—A Blueprint for the Future, para. 35. July, 1970.

metropolitan areas is to be entrusted to district authorities consisting on the one hand of existing boroughs, and on the other hand of rural districts ranging in population down to 40 000, this is what planning will continue to mean in practice throughout by far the greater part of England.

At a structure-planning level it will doubtless be recognized, at least in theory, that the control of land-use by reference to a development plan is only one of many policy instruments for securing the implementation of a plan—a negative instrument, largely ineffective where the pressure for change is strong, and of diminishing importance in relation to the positive inducement or promotion of development—and that the plan itself must be concerned as much with transportation and capital investment as it is with land-use, much more with the accommodation of growth and change than with the protection of amenity, and at least as much with the social and economic development of the community involved as with its physical environment. All this, indeed, is expressed or implied in the official documentation of the purposes of the 1968 Town and Country Planning Act. But the extent to which this concept is realized in practice will vary greatly from one part of the country to another. Where, as in the proposed West Scotland Region, the planning authority's area is virtually self-contained in respect of all the major activity systems to be accommodated, no difficulty will arise; but where, as in the existing and proposed administrative county of Cheshire, it consists of parts of the outer zones of three such units, it will not be structurally plannable. And if such instruments for the positive restructuring of the urban settlement pattern as water supply, sewerage, house-building and the creation of new towns within commuting range of major centres are to be denied to structure-planning authorities, the recent reshaping of our planning system will have little practical effect.

For the purposes of this chapter it is important also to distinguish between structural planning and what is variously called corporate planning, local government policy planning or urban management—the system whereby a local authority acts as a unity instead of as a bundle of more or less autonomous functional committees, analyses the whole range of its community's needs, determines policy objectives and priorities, formulates a comprehensive programme and concerts all its operational activities in furtherance of that programme.[1] Because the emergence of this concept of the central purpose of local government coincided with a broadening of the scope of its planning function (and because both were called 'planning'), the two developments have tended to become confused. Town and country planning was first broadened into land-use/transportation planning and then into the planning of community development—of the making of changes in the community's physical, social and economic environment. This made it an integral part of corporate planning (see Donnison, Chapter Six, page 96), but not its equivalent. Community development remains distinct from the other comprehensive function of local government, community care—the making of the best use of the community's existing equipment. It can, indeed, appropriately and with advantage be entrusted to a different level of local government.

Thus when a first-tier authority takes to corporate planning, it will find that its central policy committee and chief executive will need the assistance of a development officer who (like the finance officer and the legal officer) will be concerned with its whole range of action. He will also have to supervise all the functional departments operating in the environmental field, focusing their contributions to the policy plan and overseeing the execution of their parts of the resulting development programme. But among these departments there will still have to be a planning department, responsible for translating the relevant aspects of the policy plan into the statutory form of a structure plan, for working out action area plans within this framework, for designing (or approving) local plans, and for ensuring that major private developments are controlled accordingly. It is with the involvement of the public in the work of this department, and with its counterparts (where they exist) in second-tier authorities, that this chapter must be primarily concerned.

This is not to say that public participation should—or can—be departmentalized. Long before policy planning was thought

---

[1] For a fuller explanation of this distinction, see J. D. Stewart and Tony Eddison, 'Structure Planning and Corporate Planning', *Journal of the Royal Town Planning Institute*, Sept/Oct, 1971.

of, such pioneers of public involvement as the Coventry Planning Department were being embarrassed by the public's insistence on discussing things like street lights, dustbins and kerbs (which were none of the department's business) at meetings called to elicit contributions to the planning process. Means must be found to enlist—and satisfy—the active interest of the citizen in all aspects of the local authority's work. But the means must be apt to the purpose.

Until the 1968 Act began to take effect, the only statutory provision for public involvement in the planning process was the public inquiry into objections to a plan or into an appeal against a development control decision. This device has come to be used for at least five distinct and often mutually incompatible purposes. Its original purpose, and the only one for which it is appropriate, was to enable the responsible minister to discharge an administrative duty—the duty to decide whether to approve or amend a plan, or whether a proposed development conformed with the public interest in the proper use of land—with full knowledge of the relevant local considerations. The presiding inspector was therefore simply a reporter, and his recommendation (if any) simply an evaluation of the balance of local interest and opinion, to be weighed by the minister against other material factors and wider policy implications. But over the years the public inquiry has been required to serve as a makeshift substitute for a number of disparate requirements.

The first is a system of administrative law to safeguard private rights and interests against the abuse of administrative power. In order to appease this need without actually meeting it, the appellate inquiry has been allowed to usurp the function it was designed to subserve. In the name of 'fairness' and 'openness', ministers have acquiesced in a progressive curtailment of their discretionary power to reject their inspectors' recommendations, to the point where the time and trouble entailed in exercising it have become almost prohibitive; while third parties have been given unrestricted opportunities to have their say, or to hire lawyers to have it for them.

This has given the lawyers a chance to bend the public inquiry still further from its proper purpose—to make it serve also as a substitute for an extension of the law of nuisance. If your neighbour prevents you from enjoying your garden by

burning discarded motor tyres in his, you can seek an injunction
or damages in a court of law. If Parliament (or the judges)
decided that you had as much right to unobstructed sunshine
as to unpolluted air, they could make the same remedy available
against the building of a block of flats in your neighbour's
garden. But the lawyers find it easier to argue this sort of case
at a public inquiry—though the opportunity does not arise
unless permission is refused by the local planning authority or
the application is called in by the minister. This transforms the
inquiry from a forum for the ascertainment of the public
interest into a tribunal for the settlement of issues of right and
justice between private property owners. Its procedure has
accordingly been judicialized to such an intimidating extent
that even one of the Secretary of State's own decision officers,
attending an appellate inquiry as a third party, found that 'I for
one could not have risen to my feet to speak'.[1]

Successive ministers have leaned over backwards to indulge
this trend, ultimately to the point of abdicating their responsibility for making the final decision in respect of the small-scale
developments which account for the great majority of planning
appeals. Thereby the Government itself has finally confirmed
the popular misconception of the inspector as a judge and of
his recommendation as a verdict—and incidentally destroyed
whatever value the appellate inquiry had as a means of public
involvement in the planning process.

We have no machinery for continuous planning on a regional
scale, and therefore no frame of reference for the making of
locational decisions of more than local importance; and here
again the public inquiry has been pressed into service as a
substitute. In its statutory form, as prescribed for this purpose
in the 1968 Planning Act, the 'special inquiry commission' has
yet to be tried out; but the Roskill Commission on the Third
London Airport may fairly be regarded as its prototype. Here
the issue to be decided was one of location, and nothing but
location: as such it was wholly and solely a planning issue, and
all the relevant considerations—aeronautical, agricultural,
economic, environmental, ornithological and what-have-you—

---

[1] Pamela Payne, 'Planning Appeals', *Journal of the Royal Town Planning
Institute*, March 1971.

were in this context equally planning considerations. Yet Roskill, reporting on behalf of the majority of his colleagues, repeatedly represented the issue as a matter of judgement between economic and management advantages on the one hand and 'planning and environmental' factors on the other. As the R.I.B.A. Journal commented, 'to the very end he failed to grasp that he was heading a planning inquiry'.[1] And so ingrained in legal minds is now the notion that any public inquiry, albeit purely investigatory, must be a matter of testing and weighing 'evidence' by reference to established law, policy and precedent, that one of the most eminent lawyers practising in the planning field could subsequently justify the appointment of a high court judge to this position precisely on the principle of 'horses for courses'.[2] The eventual outcome, of course, was a triumph not in any sense for planning over jurisprudence, or even for sentiment over economics, but for public protest over professionalism.

Finally, another kind of public planning inquiry is beginning to be used as a substitute for any properly constituted machinery for public participation in the structure-planning process. Here again the new legislation has yet to be tested, but the Greater London Development Plan is the closest approximation to a structure plan so far produced, and the G.L.D.P. Inquiry must presumably be regarded as an experimental model for the structure-plan inquiries of the future.[3] It attempted to combine two elements—a conventional public inquiry by an inspector into objections to the plan, and an investigatory inquiry by a panel of experts into the plan itself. And it proved beyond question that these two elements are immiscible. The first compelled the G.L.C. to entrench itself against all-comers behind an almost meaningless written statement, while the

---

[1] *R.I.B.A. Journal*, February 1971.
[2] E. A. Vaughan-Neil at R.I.B.A.–T.C.P.A. Conference on Planning by Judicial Inquiry, April 1971.
[3] Clause 3 of the Town and Country Planning (Amendment) Bill, introduced since this chapter was written, replaces the public inquiry into objections to a structure plan with a public 'examination' of such matters affecting the Secretary of State's consideration of it as he considers ought to be so examined. It makes no provision for any discussion of alternative policies before the planning authority has made its choice.

second required it to produce a torrent of policy revisions and supporting analyses of more up-to-date information. Meanwhile the would-be participator had to specify exactly which words in the written statement he would like to see amended, and how; to submit to the scoring of debating points by the G.L.C.'s counsel on the basis of its latest document; and to accept a severe rebuke from the chairman if he introduced into his dialogue with the expert panel any matter not included in a written submission lodged a fortnight in advance.

It is, of course, essential that property-owners and other interested parties should be given an opportunity to make known and understood their objections to a new-style *local* plan, which, by showing what is proposed on an ordnance survey base, will enable its effect on the future use and value of particular holdings to be more or less accurately assessed. For this purpose it will continue to be necessary to hold an old-style public inquiry when the local plan has been completed and submitted for approval. But such an inquiry will not serve its purpose unless it is held by an inspector responsible to a higher authority endowed with power to reject or amend the plan; hence the need to have local plans prepared by metropolitan or county districts of a competent scale, subject to the *approval* of the structure-planning authority. It is, however, more than questionable whether there is any point in also holding a statutory public inquiry into objections to a *structure* plan, which will consist only of a statement of 'policy and general proposals' whose diagrammatic illustrations will not indicate how any individual plot will be affected. But what certainly will be needed, as a statutory stage in the preparation or revision of a structure plan, is some form of organized discussion of structural issues and documented alternative policies, to be held before the planning authority has made its choice. This 'statutory conference', as Peter Self has called it, must involve the structure planners, interested and disinterested pressure groups and individuals and knowledgeable advisers of the responsible government department. (Professor Self suggested that the government appointees should then issue a report, in the light of which the planning authority would complete its plan and the minister would judge it; but whether this would derogate too much from the local planning authority's proper responsibility is a matter for argument.)[1] Where a local plan is made by a district authority, subject to approval by the structure-planning authority, the same kind of procedure will be required (in addition to the local inquiry into objections to the completed plan), but in this case appointees of the structure-planning authority would take the place of the government representatives.

The 1968 Planning Act marks a considerable advance on earlier enactments in that it recognizes public participation as a necessary part of the plan-making process, and as one that is quite distinct from the ventilation of objections to the proposals of a completed plan. But the provisions actually made for this purpose in the Act and its subservient Regulations fall a long way short of what was contemplated in the preliminary White Paper and spelt out by the Skeffington Committee in *People and Planning*.[2] A more liberal attitude may be found reflected in the government's 'circular of advice' on this subject, which was still awaited at the time this chapter was written; meanwhile it is clear that all the local planning authority will be *obliged* to do in this direction is

1. to 'take such steps as will in their opinion secure' that adequate publicity is given to the report of survey and to 'the matters they propose to include in the plan', and that people who may be expected to want to make representations on these matters are made aware of their rights and given an adequate opportunity to do so;

2. to consider the representations so made and to consult the council of any affected county district, together with 'such other authorities or bodies as the local planning authority think appropriate or the Secretary of State may direct', before finally determining the content of the plan; and

3. to tell the Secretary of State what steps they have taken to comply with these requirements.

There is no guarantee that such consultations and 'consideration of the views expressed' will take place at a formative stage

---

[1] P. J. O. Self at R.I.B.A.–T.C.P.A. Conference on Planning by Judicial Inquiry, April 1971.

[2] *People and Planning*, H.M.S.O., 1969.

E

in the plan-making process, or will enable the resulting proposals to be influenced by the people whose lives they will affect. The plan may be cut and dried before they begin, so long as the planning authority does not formally adopt it until the prescribed actions have been performed.

This kind of public involvement comes only half-way up Arnstein's eight-rung ladder of 'citizen participation', which ascends from 'manipulation' to 'citizen control'.[1] It will not long satisfy the mounting demand for effective recognition of the right of ordinary people to 'say what sort of community they want and how it should develop' (Skeffington). For it is already evident that a radical change in the politics of planning is bursting upon us no less portentously than the change in our concept of planning's scope and purpose, though official thinking has lagged much further behind it.

It does not follow, however, that we in Britain should or will copy those American cities where self-constituted neighbourhood councils have wrested the initiative in making and implementing local plans from the municipal authorities by exploiting the 'maximum feasible participation' condition attaching to the distribution of grants under the 'Model Cities' and 'Community Action' programmes of the Federal Government. We can make a better job of it within our more comprehensive statutory planning system by adapting and extending our very different democratic institutions, rather than by superseding them with communes whose purview cannot comprehend the problems that most severely affect their local environment and living conditions. But we shall not succeed without drastic (and in some quarters painful) adjustments in our habits of thought.

We must first distinguish, much more clearly than did the Skeffington Committee, between public participation properly so-called (the taking of a share in the making of planning decisions by the people living in the area planned) and public relations (the winning of public support for the completed official plan). Both are necessary, but neither can take the place of the other. It is because would-be participants are so often

---

[1] S. R. Arnstein, 'A Ladder of Citizen Participation', *Journal of American Institute of Planners*, July 1969, p. 176.

fobbed off with public relations exercises that these have fallen into unmerited disrepute, especially in America. Effective arrangements for enlisting public co-operation in the making of a plan can indeed greatly ease the later task of 'selling' it, since many groundless fears will have been allayed and many active participants will feel that the plan is in some sense their own; but any plan to accommodate growth and change must hurt or threaten the interests of a substantial minority, and however generous the compensation provisions may be, its full and smooth implementation will still depend on skilled efforts to inform, enlighten and persuade the public. The Skeffington Report could hardly be faulted in what it had to say about the use of a battery of techniques for this indispensable (and in itself highly respectable) operation. Where it went sadly wrong was in regarding the final stage of the plan-formulation process (the 'statement of preferred proposals'), instead of the preceding stage ('identification of choices available'), as 'the main occasion for public participation'. From the moment when the planning authority decides which of the available options it prefers, any ostensible consultation of the public falls into the category of public relations. It is not converted into an exercise in participation merely by labelling the expository document 'for discussion'.

With this distinction clear in our minds, we can now confront the mental obstacles to real public participation. First, how can it be reconciled with the responsibility of the councillor, in a representative form of local democracy, for the making of final decisions? This is a difficulty of which councillors themselves, and such eminent legal advisers of councillors as Sir Desmond Heap, are particularly conscious; but it also has a subconscious influence on the public at large. Some 40 000 Manchester slum-dwellers would now be living in a new town at Mobberley in Cheshire if the City Council, having got Ministerial permission to build it from Lord (then Mr.) Silkin, had been able to induce as many as five per cent of its electors to vote in the poll that followed a town's meeting at which opponents of an unrelated minor clause in the same Private Bill had rejected the new town project for good measure. What kept people at home was not so much apathy as resentment at being called upon to decide such an issue: 'What else do we elect them for?' was the general attitude.

The second major obstacle is professionalism. In the minds of many practitioners of the old school, planning (like medicine) is a sophisticated professional expertise, a mystery beyond the layman's ken: the planner's job is to give his employing authority the best advice, not to do anything so unprofessional as to curry public favour for it, and if people do not like the result, their proper remedy lies in the ballot box or the public inquiry. It is further objected, by planners and others, that any genuine attempt to publicize options 'might confuse the public' (Skeffington), cause unnecessary 'blight', and prolong the already too protracted plan-making process.

All these difficulties are resolved as soon as it is recognized, first, that the only kind of planning decision which the citizen is competent to take—and which he alone is competent to take—is the selection and ordering of goals and objectives; second, that it is only when the available options are presented to him in the form of alternative hypothetical (conceptual) plans, *with a clear explanation of what each implies in terms of the subordination of one objective to another*, that the citizen can effectively exercise his right to take such decisions; third, that the expression, in conceptual-plan form, of the spatial implications of alternative ways of accommodating the ascertained needs within the operative constraints is in any case an essential phase in the evolution of a plan: fourth, that this presentation of all feasible alternatives spreads 'blight' so thinly as to make it negligible; and finally, that having produced his alternative conceptual plans, the planner must in any case spend a long time in testing them out on the ground, evaluating their local impact and carrying out the further local researches which this exercise shows to be required. If, in the meanwhile, the conceptual plans are also being evaluated by the people affected in terms of the relative acceptability of the different sets of goals they represent, no time at all will have been lost. When the upshot of this evaluation has been fed, together with the planners' own further research findings and evaluations, into the process of firming up the two most promising alternatives, it will then be for the citizens' elected representatives to decide which allocation of available resources will most effectively and economically express the known aspirations and priorities of the people concerned.

The first of these vital points calls for some elaboration.

Twenty or so years ago the planner could take his goals and objectives for granted. It did not need the arrogance of a Lord Reith to hold these truths to be self-evident: that green belts and new towns and slum clearance and taking the work to the workers were Good Things. Patrick Abercrombie, the least arrogant of post-war planners, had no fear of contradiction when he wrote in the foreword to his Greater London Plan:

> Give a man and his wife a first-rate house, a community and occupation of various kinds reasonable near at hand, within a regional framework which enables them to move freely and safely about, to see their friends and enjoy the advantages of London; add to these a wide freedom of choice and they will not grumble in the years immediately following the war.[1]

Ten years later, when an unexpected population explosion had set in and the agricultural interests ruled the roost, architects and sociologists were proclaiming with equal confidence the superior virtues of 'urbanity', high density and extended family. The prescription was reversed, but the professional's right to prescribe remained unchallenged, while the scope and social impact of planning had increased. It took a lawyer, Justice Scarman, to point out where this conjunction of professional elitism and impending omnicompetence would lead to. Addressing the Town Planning Institute in 1962—long before the P.A.G. Report—he said:

> The more fundamental one's thinking becomes, the more embracing becomes the scope of one's planning, until the ultimate absurdity is reached: having started as a planner of the use of land, one ends up planning the life of the community. Here is a trend . . . which I venture to suggest the general public fears and abhors. . . . If planning is to survive, ultimately the planner in his work must accept the standards and values of the society he serves. . . . Your task is to inform, to point consequences, to formulate alternatives; but not . . . to determine for society its values and standards.[2]

The validity of this judgement has become increasingly apparent to the planners as their technology has become more

---

[1] Patrick Abercrombie: *Greater London Plan*, 1945.
[2] Justice Scarman, 'Town and Country Planning and the Public', *T.P.I. Journal*, July/Aug. 1962.

refined and abstruse, and as the policy-making of their employing authorities has become more comprehensive and more
purposefully organized. Soul-searching humility was out of
place when all they had to do was to improve on some univers-
ally disliked effects of market forces on our physical environment. But now that they see themselves becoming able to steer
the whole course of a community's development by means
which laymen cannot understand, they feel a need to be told
which port people want them to make for. They must still use
their own informed judgement when they are planning new
developments for an unknown clientele, and they must always
bear in mind that the outcome of their efforts will also have to
serve a generation yet unborn; but as their work becomes
increasingly concerned with the renewal of long-established
settlements, and especially of the inner urban areas predominantly occupied by the most disadvantaged elements of our
society, they are becoming increasingly conscious of the limitations, as guides to what they should seek to achieve, of their
own middle-class values, of the results of elections and of the
findings of social surveys. And the more positive and sensitive
their command of the means to reach given objectives, the
more acutely they feel the need to be briefed by their client
communities.

Pressure groups on behalf of sectional interests are always
with us, but they never add up to a sounding-board for the
community as a whole. Yet it is only in response to pressures
of one sort or another that our governors can bring themselves
to make the marginal adjustments of established policies and
programmes which are the stuff of democratic government.
Therefore planners, elected or professional, who want to be
able to use their power and skill in the general interest of their
community as a whole, need not only a reliable way of identifying community aims but also the backing of organized community pressures for their attainment.

Yet it is no use just to invite people to express their value
judgements by listing abstract social goals (privacy, sociability)
or specific resource objectives (better housing, access to town
centre) in order of preference, and then to expect policies based
on the apparent outcome to be accepted as a true reflection
of community aims. It is only when people can see the feasible
options embodied in changes in an environment they know, and

so can realize how these changes will affect the activities they want to pursue, that they can make their value judgements understood. Hitherto they have been able to do this only when the changes have been implemented; then the planners have found to their pained surprise that not all their well-meant efforts are appreciated—often, no doubt, because they have failed to take account of economic and social as well as physical and financial constraints, but nearly always because they have also misconceived the values of the people they were planning for.

How far the professional planner as such should seek to modify economic and social constraints through the redistribution of power and wealth, or should leave this to his elective counterpart, may be open to argument. But it is clear that a major part of his function as a planner will in future be to catalyse the manifestation of his community's political and social values, in time to enable them to shape planning policies, by postulating alternative solutions and explaining their value implications.[1]

There has been heartening evidence[2] that practising planners, chartered or not, are now prepared thus to become at the same time humbler and more effective servants of their communities. There has been even more heartening evidence that local councillors are beginning to get the message too, in spite of its apparent threat to existing institutions of representative democracy. In 1971, for example, Islington Borough Council invited the inhabitants of an area which it thought should be wholly redeveloped to decide whether a quarter, a half, or three-quarters should instead be rehabilitated—and accepted their verdict in favour of three-quarters. And Camden Borough Council confronted visitors to a municipal exhibition with various quantities of environmental goodies, each appropriately priced, together with a limited number of counters to 'spend' on their preferred selection. No doubt the primary object was to impress on the public the harsh realities of economic

---

[1] For a slightly different interpretation of this prospect, see G. P. Cherry, *Official Architecture and Planning*, March 1971.

[2] Notably in F. J. C. Amos's Presidential Address to the R.T.P.I., October 1971.

resource allocation, but the feedback to the council and its planning staff was no less valuable. A development of this 'priority evaluator' could easily be used in conjunction with a series of alternative conceptual plans to reveal what the goals and objectives of the final plan ought to be.

It will not be enough, however, that planning authorities should voluntarily seek to educate and consult the people affected by their plans. Community participation will have to be recognized as a right and given an appropriate power-base, within the hierarchy of our democratic institutions, from which grass-roots values can effectively be brought to bear on local bureaucracies—and on the wielders of influence whom local bureaucracies must heed. Every community, urban or rural, which recognizes itself as such, will have to be allowed to elect a neighbourhood or parish council, with power to raise revenue and spend it on any communal need which no other body has a statutory duty to supply, and with the right to be consulted in good time by the local plan-making authority and any other public body whose development proposals may affect the local environment. This is a claim which government and munici- palities alike are as yet reluctant to admit, but one which cannot long be appeased by the toleration or encouragement of voluntary community associations and civic societies with no elective status or statutory resources.

It is important to keep clear the distinction in *kind* between such a neighbourhood or parish council and an administrative local authority, whatever its scale. To serve its essential purpose, a neighbourhood or parish council must represent a real community of place—an area to which people *feel* they belong, and not merely one whose inhabitants share an objective community of interest. It has been clearly established[1] that the scale of such communities is everywhere much too small to enable them to run statutory services of their own, or even to serve as the basis for the smallest operational units of the local authority's personal services. The existence of such councils would not diminish the need to make the scale of the authority responsible for the day-to-day administration of the personal

---

[1] *Community Attitudes Survey*, Research Studies 9, Royal Commission on Local Government in England, H.M.S.O., 1969.

services (including health) as small as is consistent with their functional effectiveness, and to decentralize their field operations to combined local centres on the lines proposed by Donnison in Chapter Six. Neither would the constitution of district authorities at the minimum population levels proposed in the White Paper[1] on Local Government in England do anything to lessen the need for neighbourhood and parish councils.

That need is precisely the same in rural districts, boroughs and metropolitan districts. It is also precisely the same in the deprived inner city ghetto, the middle-class suburb and the stockbroker's village—though the use made of a community council's influence and resources will obviously differ according to the nature of its problems. Each may be preoccupied with a matter that can properly be settled only by an authority extensive enough to comprehend the whole of the issue involved —be it overcrowded slums in the ghetto, the routing of an urban motorway through the suburb or the reception of over-spill in the village. But each has the same right to determine its own social values, to have them properly appreciated wherever decisions affecting its community are taken and to decide for itself anything which concerns only its own community. To deny the case for neighbourhood councils in privileged areas on the ground that support for it does not help the cause of social equality, and may distract attention from it, makes no more sense than to oppose or neglect cancer research on the same ground.

On the other hand there will, of course, be a continuing need for special assistance to the deprived areas, preferably channelled through their neighbourhood councils, as well as an obligation to give due priority to their needs in all plans and programmes for the development of wider areas—as the Strategy for the South East did, but the G.L.D.P. failed to do. An important element in this special assistance will be the training of neighbourhood council members and other community leaders—not in the principles or the technology of planning, but in political organization, in the rules of the power

---

[1] Cmnd. 4584, para. 34. The 'normal' range of population size for county districts has since been set at 75–100 000.

game and in the techniques of securing attention and respect for their community's own self-determined goals.

Elective, revenue-raising neighbourhood councils, then, are indispensable to effective public participation in the planning process in suburban and inner-city areas alike. But that is not to say that they would of themselves achieve this purpose in the inner-city areas, or would be welcomed and used for this purpose by the community action groups that have latterly sprung up in such areas. Still less is it to say that they would help to remedy the economic deprivations and social injustices with which these groups are rightly preoccupied. All the major problems of the inner-city areas demand for their solution a massive transfer of resources from the suburban and exurban parts of the same regional communities, and the only kind of local government organization that could materially contribute to such a solution would be an authority of at least city-region scale. In the absence of such authorities, community action groups in inner-city areas are bound to feel that their only hope lies in bypassing local government and appealing directly to the concern (sympathetic or apprehensive) of central government. From their point of view, what little a neighbourhood council can do to improve the local environment, either directly or by exerting pressure on a council whose jurisdiction is confined to the city (or even to the conurbation), represents only a diversion of effort from much more important objectives. They are not interested in getting the priorities right among the merely environmental goals which it lies within the power of the local planning authority to attain: to them, public participation—indeed planning itself—is simply an irrelevance.

In the United States, where local government is hopelessly fragmented, this lesson has already been learnt by bitter experience: 'citizen participation' is now a dirty phrase in Harlem and Detroit. In Britain it is still politically possible for us to give local government the power, the financial resources and the structural capacity to cope with the social, economic and environmental problems of the region-wide communities our great cities have become. We could thereby create a context in which the planning of land-use, transportation and investment in physical development might effectively subserve comprehensive policies for the enhancement of the quality of life, and might itself be guided by a meaningful expression of each local community's value judgements. What we do with this opportunity will set the limits to what planning can achieve during the remainder of this century, for it is an opportunity which cannot be expected to recur for at least fifty years. At the time these words are being written we are, so far as the major metropolitan regions of England are concerned, in process of throwing it away.

Chapter Eight

Planning and the Market

CHRISTOPHER FOSTER

It is often said that in the past the rôle of the market has not been emphasized enough in physical planning and that it should be considered more. It is almost as if it was thought there were two sets of forces acting independently—market forces and the initiatives taken by planners. One supposes there are several reasons for this. While in many other countries— from the United States to underdeveloped nations—the interests of local politicians and a concentration of attention on economic growth have forced physical planners to put the stimulation of industry and employment at the top of their priorities, physical planners in Britain have been readier and more able to accept these outside factors which are given to them. The stimulation of local employment and policy towards depressed areas has been the subject of governmental regional policy which still has very little to do with physical planning, either intellectually or institutionally. For the most part planners have not felt that the welfare of industry and business had much to do with them, and they have not normally related what they were doing to economic objectives, for example not many can have asked how their redevelopment schemes, housing, or use of planning regulations in their area, were likely to affect local real income per head or its distribution. Certainly it is hard to think of any case until recently where any formal analysis has been made on these lines.

There are many reasons why this separation of physical and economic objectives is beginning to break down, but among the most important is the realization that physical planners, even when backed by politicians, cannot always impose their will. If planners make a plan which happens to be disliked, say by a firm or a landlord, these do not simply submit but take evasive action. When planners impose constraints on their action, they tend to substitute new courses of action for old. Thus, certain building regulations stimulate ingenuity in finding loop-holes; or industries prevented from using locations they prefer will not always tamely go where the planners want but will move elsewhere. To take a more complex example, physical planners were anxious for green belts round cities to serve recreational and aesthetic purposes, but they did not anticipate—as economics would have suggested to them—that this would have the effect of raising land prices throughout the city with consequences that many disliked. The point is that the market is not to be ordered around. Whatever planners may do, economic agents pursue their own goals, doing the best they can in their own interests given the constraints that planners and others impose on them. It was not unknown for planners to react by piling on more regulations and restrictions in the hope of making their objectives dominant. Given statutory and political support, this may often be possible, but usually the cost of such drastic policies begin to become apparent. Property developers, landlords and industry begin to complain that whatever it is that planners may wish to achieve may not be worth the costs of pursuing such policies, and opposition builds up.

Neither, frequently, does it appear to the planners that their own objectives are being achieved. They find themselves wrestling with market forces which are often stronger than they are. If they try to 'allow' for the forces of the market in their own planning, they may face the accusation that the same ends could have been achieved with less trouble if they had not bothered to intervene. If they persist, they will run into the argument which has so often been advanced against *dirigiste* Soviet and other socialist planners who have tried to control an economy, that the wasteful confusion of objectives and sheer inefficiency that results is again worse than if there had been no intervention.

There are so many cases one could cite where planning does not seem to have worked. While housing queues have been eliminated in some areas, this has not been where the queues are longest; and while there is an element of tautology in this, it is true that where housing need has generally been defined to be the greatest, there has been least success in meeting it. This has been largely through the interaction of other competing demands for land and subsidized housing. Moreover, as is notorious, public housing has tended not to help the poorest, mainly because subsidizing the housing needs of the less poor has until recently deterred them from moving into the private housing market. Thus upward filtering has not worked. Also striving after relatively high Parker Morris housing standards has made it difficult for poor people to afford good public housing, even at current (subsidized) council rents. Quite other examples are the existence of council shopping developments which have turned out to be very slow to let because shopkeepers were not attracted to them, or of public housing estates remote from shops because shopkeepers did not find it profitable to move into the shops provided.

None of this, however, is an argument for saying that one should stop planning and leave urban development to the market, unless one believes that the inefficiency and waste of planning is inevitably so great as to make it less effective than the operations of an imperfect market. There are strong arguments for *some* planning, if it is efficient and designed to achieve its objectives. There is as much danger in some circles in Britain of underestimating the potential efficiency of the market, as there is in exaggerating it in others. There is a tendency for those who like existing trends—for example, the decentralization of large cities—to argue that it is consistent with the market, as there is for those who dislike it to see it as something needing to be corrected by planning. But the truth is that what goes on in our cities is a sad tangle of planning intervention and other forces, so that it is impossible—at least without better data and more powerful techniques than have been used so far—to determine causation. All one can say is that in principle there is a good theoretical case for some planning.

Economists have their habits like everyone else, and often start a discussion by asking why events cannot be left to themselves. This has its roots in the *laisser-faire* origins of the subject. Most economists at one time did believe that national wealth would be greatest if governments did not intervene in the free workings of the markets, except in a few carefully circumscribed rôles. Nowadays a disposition towards *laisser faire* is more often a gesture of despair. While government interventions could improve matters from a number of standpoints, the best of government intentions so often have muddled and harmful consequences that the market is best left to itself. Even so, there are many economists who are less sceptical of the benefits of government intervention than this. But one does not have to believe dogmatically or sceptically in *laisser faire* to find it useful to begin an analysis by asking why intervention is desirable. If we ask what difference interventionist policies may make to the operation of market forces, it is easier to define the objectives of such policies and tests of their success and failure. Ultimately, we surely want intervention to be justified by works, not by faith. It also emphasizes that those who plan intervention must reckon that the market will react to such intervention, and will do what it can to minimize its effects where these impose costs on agents in the market. There is what is now called 'feedback' between intervention and the market.

Planning may be defined as one form of intervention by governments in the urban process. There are cities in the world where governments take little interest in the land and building markets, or in the development of land use, and where nothing we would recognize as town, or physical, planning exists. The governments of such countries may be far from *laisser faire* in relation to other policies, but in their urban policies they are. The effort of imagination an economist tries to make is to consider what would happen in a city if there were no intervention by the planner, and evaluate the planning there is by comparison with a 'no planning' policy. This chapter is such an economist's approach to planning and the market.

In the economic textbooks which described the workings of a free market under perfect competition, there was always an assumption made that all those involved in the market—the buyers and sellers—had 'perfect knowledge'. If they were to achieve their own self-interest, they needed sufficient knowledge. This did not have to be omniscience, but enough data about their customers, suppliers and competitors to make rational decisions, in possession of the relevant facts. In many markets, the agents have satisfactory sources of information of their own, but where information is deficient, there is at least a *prima facie* case for governments intervening to provide better data for better decision-making. This is a stronger case in the urban market than in many others. Many urban decisions are made by, or affect, individuals who cannot be expected to have acquired the knowledge or the expertise to analyse their predicament. They have to decide where to buy a house or rent a small shop, or how to react to developments around them which may affect the value of their house or business. While larger firms, trade unions and other organizations may be expected to have acquired the knowledge and expertise to cope with their ordinary decisions, many of their most important 'urban' decisions are made only a few times in their lifetime: a decision whether or not to relocate, and where to go, can be well outside the experience of even a large firm. It could quite easily make an inferior decision because of limited knowledge of the relevant facts. Moreover, learning from one's own mistakes is often exceptionally costly in an urban situation. While a dissatisfied buyer of clothes or a dishwasher can resolve never to go to the same shop, someone who buys a house and finds it is badly placed for jobs and schools, may be effectively locked in for many years because of all the costs, financial and subjective, of making another move.

One would expect a rapid growth in profit-making organizations to provide information for such decisions. Some exist. Developers and large companies often have their own information systems. Consultants exist to help firms with their location problems, though they have specialized mostly in helping firms to decide in what town to locate, rather than where in a given city. If one is rich enough, one can hire people to help one choose a house, though their advice is also usually limited to finding a house of given physical specifications in a 'desirable' neighbourhood. In future one may expect them to advise more on the environmental characteristics of a house: the social-demographic description of the population; accessibility to shops which are cheap or of high quality; accessibility to job opportunities for the housewife; the incidence of pollution in the area and how this is likely to be affected by nearby changes in industrial land-use, or the build-up of vehicles on main roads; decibel counts and how these too are likely to be affected by developments in the neighbourhood; the scholastic achievements of neighbourhood schools as well as data on the kind of children they turn out; even, possibly, the performance and achievements of the local doctors. People are waking up to a realization how much such decisions may affect their happiness, their income-earning opportunities and the appreciation of their capital, perhaps because of greater mobility, but also because larger cities tend towards providing more differentiated 'packages' which people can buy into, than did cities a few decades ago. Not only is there the difference between living in the city centre and in the suburbs or exurbs, but the suburbs and exurbs have their differences also. In the past people have tended to make such decisions on what is often called a 'green fingers' approach. They dash round the neighbourhoods keeping their eyes open, but for people, as for firms, more of these decisions may become too complex for such an approach to be satisfying; hence the growth of specialist providers of such information.

Why cannot provision of such information be left entirely to private enterprise? First, the services are likely to be built up originally to inform those who have most to lose financially from bad decision-making and can afford to pay. But it may be less profitable to provide such information for ordinary home-owners and small shopkeepers. There may therefore be a case for the local authority acting as a kind of consumers' association or council for the small man and the small firm. Second, one reason why these information services have been slow to develop is because of the size of the investment needed to assemble the data and then update it. If one private organization does it, this is a disincentive to others to copy it. The chances are that in most cities there will be someone with a monopoly for providing such information, with all the problems of abuse and control that follow. This is an argument for the local authority being the provider of that information at least where collection and updating costs are particularly high. Third, much of the information the consumers of such services would like is normally thought to be confidential. Much of the data which broadly characterizes a neighbourhood socially is available on a small area basis from the Census of Population. The characterization of a street or the evaluation of a group of shops could probably be achieved without noticeable invasion of privacy, but there is always the risk that such information services could be tempted towards collection of information which might seem like an invasion of privacy. This might be an argument for government to impose constraints on the collection of information, or for governments to collect some of it themselves on the grounds that their officials would be responsible and law-abiding in its use. Fourth, some of the relevant information would have its source in local government anyway. Some of this relates to matters where government initiates and decides change: highway and school planning and, in general, the planning of urban public services; some relates to areas where changes in policies may be influential. It is arguable that local government should disseminate this data directly to all who want it rather than through the intermediacy of profit-making firms. Fifth, and most important of all, is the danger that services providing information on a profit-making basis will not stop at that, but will be tempted to influence events through the information they provide to their own profit. They could become speculators in land or property, or the instruments of such speculators, when their first loyalty would no longer be providing honest, dispassionate data to their customers. Given the probability of monopoly, there is surely a great possibility of abuse.

That providing information is a legitimate activity of planning departments is witnessed by the recent growth of reports and statistical information provided by them. Plans themselves are such information. The new-style structure plans, continuously updated, are a further move towards providing more relevant information, or ought to be. As so often with governments, the usefulness of all this for the ordinary citizen and the ordinary firm is limited by an ambivalence in the motives behind the collection and presentation of the information. The plan, and much of the other published data, may be unintelligible to most people. Much other information may be available in local authority offices to those who know it is there, but besides being practically inaccessible to the majority, its meaning is even less likely to be plain to the ordinary person. One reason for this is the sheer difficulty of expressing the information collected. An old-style plan was a 'picture' which, so far as it went, many could visualize. Visualization and visual presentation is more difficult when one is trying to describe processes over time. It is more difficult still when one is trying to present options and make significant the differences between them, or when the developments presented are strategic rather than reflected in precise changes in what is drawn on a map. Besides, what is most informative is not written down in many instances in the published documents, but is the interchange and examination of the plans recorded in the proceedings of a public inquiry.

As a result, the copious information provided by planning authorities is likely to be most meaningful to those inside the authority and those comparatively few outsiders who have a deep interest and understanding. This also implies that the larger firms and richer people are most likely to employ those who will make the most intelligent use of the data. But there is a second reason why this information is not as useful to ordinary people and firms as it could be. Most data is collected for the purposes of the local authority, for its politicians and officers to plan its services and to fulfil its statutory obligations to the Department of the Environment and others. In many cases this will have small connection with the information citizens will want for their decisions. One could argue that a local authority planning an area as suitable for private housing development ought to have taken into account all the environmental factors and social characteristics of its neighbourhood which make it suitable for that development. In practice, such market research is likely to be less complete. Thus if the local authority's planning department is to become a provider of information to help the market work more efficiently and to help all parties to make better decisions in their own interest, there must be a revolution in the principles governing the collection of data; a rethinking of the purpose it should serve. Local authorities will have to feel under a duty to present data in a form which is most useful and intelligible to the citizen for his purposes, not theirs.

In many local authorities another revolution is wanted. Many find it hard to escape distinguishing between *us* and *them*. The planner collects and presents information to do battle with *them*. First he must persuade his politicians, but thereafter why should he make life difficult by providing information for **the** *other* side—as he may see the Inspectors at a Public Inquiry, or citizens who oppose his plans outside the formal political process? And one can see why it is very difficult to ask the planner to argue both sides of the case. So what commonly happens is that the planner does not 'hide' material information, but he does not go out of his way to explain all its relevance when it might damage the local authority case. For example, he will explain that various parties have various rights of appeal against local authority plans, but he will not go out of his way to show the citizen how to make a case, or what arguments may be persuasive and what are likely to be judged irrelevant. He will not provide the information for the citizen or his advocate to make a case as well as he will provide it for his own.

The matter appears somewhat complicated. Even the most *laisser-faire* economist or politician is unlikely to deny that the urban 'market' would work more efficiently if the various parties had more information. A good argument can be put up for the intervention of the planning authority to provide more information rather than this being left entirely to private enterprise. But if the planning authority does not redefine his loyalties then the picture is far less clear. If he puts his loyalty to his political masters first, then it is arguable that the ordinary people and firms may be better off if private information services develop, despite the inclination of these to serve the better off and the possibility of abuse. An alternative is the development of independent non-profit-making organizations, as in the United States, to look after these informational needs of the citizen on a continuing basis: an intervention in the market, but not by governments.

Another area of intervention by local government, as well as by central government and by public authorities, is in the provision of urban public services. Why such services should be provided publicly raises questions of the widest scope which cannot be discussed in this chapter, and are not directly relevant to it. If these services were provided on profit-making principles so that only the fact of public ownership distinguished them from private enterprise, it might seem that we would have discovered no new rôle for the planner. Such public enterprises would find information services of the kind discussed in the last section quite as useful as large private enterprises would. It would help them decide where to locate schools, health and welfare services or how to develop sewage and public water supply systems. But essentially the rôle of the public provider in the market would be no different from that of the private firm. If they were truly commercial, they would be competing with private enterprise and each other.

One function that is coming to be seen as one of planning would exist in relation to the provision of such services. It does not involve 'intervention' as we have defined it. It is in principle no different from corporate planning practised in private enterprise. Budgeting and revenue forecasting systems are devised so that the operations of the activity can be planned. Expenditure and revenue are forecast on a number of assumptions about the future. The enterprise has one option selected for it which is judged the most profitable and plans its operations accordingly. In more refined systems, a city looks on itself so far as it can as an integrated business. It consolidates the accounts of its various operations into one. It selects a corporate plan for its future.

There is, however, one important difference between the corporate plan of a firm and of a city. No one doubts that the prominent, if not the only, purpose of the first is to maximize returns to the shareholders. There is no such simple dominating objective for the city. The formulation of a corporate plan brings out into the open the need to weight the interests of the various beneficiaries from possible alternative strategies for the future of the city. In many cases this is done—as in central government—on an *ad hoc* basis. Cost effectiveness or cost-benefit techniques are used to find the objectives of different programmes independently of each other. As in the past, judgement is used—that of politicians or officials—to switch funds at the margin between programmes. No city, to my knowledge, has gone further than this. Few have got so far. But in principle one can imagine a state of affairs where the authorities of a city are able to deploy what economists call a social welfare function or decision function. This would give explicit weight to the various interest groups within the city, and it would make clear what amalgam of efficiency and redistributive objectives the city was using.

Subject to these qualifications, the recent interest in programme budgeting and economics applied to cities, which is creeping across the Atlantic, is equivalent to a development of corporate planning for local government. One reason for this tendency is a much greater concern for efficiency in local government. Behind this is the realization, or fear, that local expenditures on public services normally seem to rise faster than *per capita* incomes, implying that if this rate of increase is to be maintained, local taxes must also rise faster than *per capita* incomes. Urban public services tend to be labour intensive. As real labour costs rise faster than the costs of most other inputs, the cost of public goods and services in cities will rise faster than those of most privately produced goods and services. While there may be economies of scale in the production of services like sewage, refuse disposal, libraries and a number of others, these are mostly related to high densities of population. Residential densities tend to fall as cities grow, and this may well raise the unit cost of providing some or all these services. At the same time as their incomes rise, citizens require larger quantities of some services—for example, of water as their standards of hygiene rise—or improved quality—for example, of schooling as their understanding of the benefits of education for their children rises. If such services were profit-making and prices rose to reflect costs, as they would if the services were supplied privately, there would be no special problem for the public-sector corporate planner.[1]

A realization of the increasing burden of financing urban services, as well as a general concern for efficiency, has led to widespread challenging of the traditional financial bases on which these services have usually been provided. These were principles by which certain standards of provision were laid down and occasionally revised upwards to reflect changing public opinion. Rapid increases in cost have made it harder for cities with fiscal problems to continue with this, and there has been a shift towards providing services on an optimizing basis. An almost equivalent way of making the same point is to note the increased interest in programme budgeting and urban economics. Whether the physical planner of the past becomes the urban corporate planner of the future is basically only a demarcation dispute and a question about who in local

---

[1] Corporate planner is used here in a sense which the author, though not necessarily his colleagues, believes to agree with usage in business and to be most useful. Corporate planning in a firm is a reaction against informal and loosely related methods of financial controls. It is essentially an examination of a number of net revenue forecasts based on alternative policies and predictions of the future. By analogy, corporate planning for a local authority is based on financial forecasts of its expenditures and revenues.

authorities will acquire, or be allowed to acquire, the new skills. But in so far as local authorities develop a corporate planning approach, this will affect the *modus operandi* of the physical planner even if we restrict his rôle to that of the provision of information. This is even more the case if there are substantial changes in policies for providing urban services, like a change from a generally satisficing to a generally optimizing approach or a change from a tradition where many services are financed from taxes and grants without much reference to the average costs of supplying the service, towards an approach where it is normal for citizens to be charged a price related to the actual costs of providing the service to them. In Britain a great many pricing policies and standards of provision have conspired to mean lower density development than otherwise would be the case (though there have been other forces like green belt policy working in the opposite direction). A marginal cost pricing policy would greatly alter the relative costs of developing at different densities. Or, to take a less academic example, the recent White Paper revolutionizing housing finance and subsidies is likely to have a profound effect, not merely on housing but on land-use development and densities. The White Paper does not mention these things but it is arguable that planners would serve their communities if they were able to revise their forecasts and their plans to reflect the land-use consequences of such policy changes. Otherwise there is the danger yet again that the best informed and wiliest will tumble to the effects soonest, to the possible disadvantage of some other citizens.

There is one distinct respect in which the rôle of the city as provider of public services may throw a special responsibility on the planner, even if we continue to think of him as purveyor of information and the city's corporate planner. The longevity of so much local public investment means that its tends to constrain the development of the city. This is most obviously true of major transport construction, but is also true of some other infrastructure. In a world of perfect competition with perfect knowledge, all the parties would be discounting the future, but they would have some opinion, backed by cash, on the future shape of the city. In practice, businessmen and home-owners may discount the future so heavily that they may have no opinions to express on events even fifteen years hence.

The consequences of alternative motorway proposals planned now, built over the next few years, but achieving their major impact more than a decade from now, may be a matter of pure indifference to them. Some of the city's inhabitants will be dead and others know that they may have moved elsewhere; it is unlikely that they will try to reflect the interests of future generations. It is arguable that the planning authorities, because they represent the city which is practically immortal, have a duty to consider the interests of future generations, properly discounted to reflect the passage of time, but otherwise with as much weight given to future generations as to the present. If this job is to be done properly, planners must begin by genuinely trying to evaluate the interests of these future generations. They must go on to consider how they will differ from the present generation in predictable characteristics such as population size, the rate of household formation, age distribution, income and, so far as possible, their propensities to spend on different groups of goods. This implies sophisticated forecasting, more market research of a different kind than is common and also controlled speculation about the future. There would seem to be little alternative except making insufficient allowance for the future or relying on the unaided intuitions of the planner to decide what future generations will want. However he does it, the rôle of the planner here is that of an advocate of interests in the future not sufficiently represented in the present; and the particular importance of this derives in our argument so far from the fact that some public investments have such longevity that they are likely to affect the interests and arrangements of future generations profoundly, even if their progenitors alive today do not appreciate it.

No *laisser-faire* economist could dispute the rôle of the planner as provider of information, though he might take a different view on the relative ability of the planner and of private enterprise to provide good information with less abuse. At an extreme, he might argue that there was little private enterprise could not provide more efficiently, but he is hardly likely to argue that the provision of unbiased and unbiasing information, if that is possible, will make the market work less efficiently. Neither, if there are local public services, is he likely to object to the planner as corporate planner, whatever he may feel about their being public rather than private. He may be doubtful about the ability of the planner to simulate the preferences of future generations, but he will probably agree there is a problem which just listening to the market will not solve.

None of this constitutes what is usually understood by intervention—which is why I have mentioned it first. Neither is it what most people think of as the main function of physical planning. It omits all reference to or defence of planning controls. Planning is usually thought of as a more positive intervention into the urban fabric. The economist considering these interventions will probably divide them into two groups to analyse them, while recognizing that many cases have attributes of both.

The first of these is market failure. For the sake of analysis we may continue to suppose that the city and the planner regard themselves primarily as a service organization to provide the services citizens want, given their ability to pay. Intervention may be justified, even so, on the grounds of promoting efficiency because the market fails to achieve the efficient solution (for some other reason than absence of sufficient information). Classically, the economist would analyse all such cases as divergences between private and social costs or benefits, or, to use a less complex expression now becoming commoner, as examples of externalities. Following convention, a *private* cost is an out-of-pocket expense by a firm, individual or other entity making a decision. A *private* benefit is revenue or income received by such entities as a result of their decisions. A *social* cost is an expense borne by anyone else as a result of such an entity's action for which they are not compensated. A *social* benefit is a gain by such an entity in similar circumstances which they do not have to forfeit. The notion of an externality is simply that a private cost or benefit is internal to the decision-maker, a social cost or benefit is *external* to him.

One kind of externality relevant to planning, and expressing market failure, is what is called an external economy, or diseconomy of scale. If a city is said to have external economies of scale, this might mean that every additional enterprise locating in a city was not only profitable in itself but increased the profits of other firms. A plausible reason for this would be an increase in specialization and the division of labour. It is often said that one of the advantages of a large city is a large, trained and versatile labour force. This is the result not only of formal education, but of several generations of on-the-job training and the handing-down of expertise from father to son. Firms in the past who have contributed to this by supplying on-the-job training have presumably found this profitable, but because there is no slavery, they cannot ensure that when they have trained a man, all the benefits accrue to them; he may walk off and join a rival who then derives a social benefit or externality. Similarly the arrival of an innovating firm with technological spin-off may stimulate other firms to innovate either in emulation or because some of the ideas trickle through. Here again the social benefit is likely to be greater than the private benefit. It is usually argued that such external economies of scale increase indefinitely with the size of the town. Some might argue that they are an almost necessary result of urban growth. But an urban planner, by a wise stimulation of industries carefully chosen, may be able to increase the value of such external economies for his city. There is a difference between this and the activity many planners undertake of persuading firms that it is in their own interests to locate in their city, since this is an information service and all that is at issue are the profits of the firm and no wider social benefit. It is these external benefits alone which, on the basis of our analysis so far, justify intervention by the planner. What form the intervention may take raises separate issues. The planner may persuade the firm by argument. However, when the social benefit exceeds the private benefit, there is a *prima facie* case for it being worth the city's while to subsidize the location of the firm providing that the social benefit expected does not exceed the cost of the subsidy. One can regard such a subsidy as an investment from which the city derives a return. It is much less obvious that it is worth the nation's while to make such a subsidy, since on the efficiency grounds with which we are now concerned, the probabilities are that a firm wishing to expand will do so in some city. If there were two cities where the external economies that would result were equal, it would be a matter of indifference to the state whether it located in one or the other. Therefore it is only in the interest of the state to subsidize such an industrial development to the extent that more external economies would result from the choice of a particular location.

A similar reason for intervention may justify many of the environmental concerns, though the argument works in reverse:

these are diseconomies, some of them external diseconomies associated apparently with city size. The classic and most frequently cited example of divergence between private and social costs is still relevant. This is the example of an industry, a gasworks or tannery for example, which pollutes the surrounding neighbourhood. The pollution is a by-product of its activities. The costs from experiencing it fall on the neighbourhood. Those who suffer are in general not entitled to compensation for it. These, then, are by definition social costs. The pollutor does not reduce or eliminate pollution because it would reduce his profits to do so. He would have to buy more costly fuel or raw materials, or install new capital equipment. If the social benefit from his doing so were greater than this cost, then it would pay society for it to happen. Given the circumstances, it will not happen through the market. It is also the case that such pollution seems to be an increasing function of city size. Pollution is affected by the kinds of industry a city possesses, the level of car ownership and climatic conditions, but the greater the volume of pollution, the progressively greater tend to be its harmful effects.

The example of pollution presents two kinds of difficulty when we relate it to the activity of the planner. The first is that the sensible course of action for a city is to decide what is the most efficient strategy against pollution. The most efficient measures will vary with the cause of pollution. In some cases— for example, controls over automobile standards—the problem can be best dealt with nationally, but there may be many other cases where it is most efficient to develop a strategy at the city level. One may then ask if it is the business of the planner, given his general concern with the environment, to initiate and develop such a strategy, or is it someone else's responsibility, and if so, whose is it? The second question is whether the interest of the physical planner in this matter is to be constrained by the nature of the instruments adopted to mitigate pollution. In some cases the most efficient solutions may involve remedies and controls which have traditionally been the concern of physical planners. The clearest example is the strong possibility that the most efficient way of dealing with some noxious industries is to zone them so that they tend to pollute each other and no one else. (In economist's language, he may or may not be interested to learn that he is creating a complex which, to the maximum efficient extent, internalizes the social costs of pollution within a group who pollute each other.) A view that a brake should be put on city size to offset external diseconomies of scale from pollution would be a traditional planning solution, and might, for example, be used to justify a green belt policy, or more direct planning controls. The difficulty here is the improbability that this is the most efficient solution to the problem. There seems more than a chance that a piecemeal approach to the various causes of solution would be preferable and would avoid any such constraint on city size. One can imagine, however, cases where the topography and climatic conditions were such as to make piecemeal solutions particularly costly, and where the most efficient solution might be a brake on the city's growth if that could be achieved.

Noise nuisance is capable of a similar analysis as a social cost inflicted by some people on others. Planners can zone or impose controls to reduce some noises, and provided the social benefit exceeds the social cost, an economist would say there is an economic justification for it, but many of the most efficient solutions to particular sources of noise lie outside the planner's function as usually conceived.

A more interesting case analytically is visual intrusion. If market forces were allowed to operate freely, one would expect a tendency for buildings to be crammed together at high densities. The first comer would buy his plot of land and build on it. The second would buy the adjacent land and would give much less weight to the interests of his neighbour; he would find it in his own interests to build his house at a density that is most likely to blanket his neighbour's view and even affect his ventilation. He is not likely to be deterred from a high plot-ratio by the thought that the next comer will perform the same trick on him, since there is no guarantee, if he is a good neighbour and considers the interest of those who arrived before him, that this will have any influence on those who arrive after him. His only effective policy is to buy a larger site than he would otherwise require in order to keep his neighbour at a distance. Thus, in such a world of market freedom, one would expect people to buy larger plots (and economize on something else). Then if the land were being developed in sequence, they would locate as near the boundary of existing neighbours as possible, leaving as much room as they can between them and the plots which the next comers will buy to develop on. At least this seems a plausible scenario. Another possibility is that such a situation makes it possible for those who come later to hold up to ransom those who came before. Rationally someone who built a house with a vacant plot next door would be prepared to pay up to his valuation of the disutility he would receive from having his vision obscured or to the point where he would rather move, whichever was the less. This is capable of being analysed as a divergence between private and social costs, but it is an example of a special case of such a divergence which seems to be of central importance for the evaluation of planning.

This particular example of market failure has been characterized by two American economists, Whinston and Davies, as the Prisoners' Dilemma. Their use of it was as a justification for urban renewal programmes, but it has much more far-reaching implications. The Dilemma itself has an older history and its provenance is American. A district attorney takes two suspects into custody. He has strong, but not conclusive, evidence that they are guilty of the same crime. He talks to each separately. They are kept in seclusion from each other. He tells them they have the choice of confessing. If neither confesses he will book both on a minor charge and they will get a short term of imprisonment. If both confess, they will get prison terms, but not the heaviest. If one confesses, he gets off free as State's evidence, while the other gets the maximum sentence. The Dilemma is that unless the two men can collude, it is rational for each man to confess. If he confesses, either the other does not, when he will get off scot free, or the other man also confesses, when both get a moderate sentence. If he does not confess, he will either get a light sentence, or the maximum. He must be better off confessing if he does not know what the other will do. If collusion were possible, then silence would be their best policy.

We will suppose there is a run-down urban area in which the properties blight each other. Once this was thought a comparatively simple problem if one had the funds: pull down and redevelop. One can only upgrade if:

1. the tenants are got rid of
2. there is a rise in their income levels so that they are prepared to pay more,

3. the landlords change their policies, or
4. there is a subsidy.

The first is of doubtful social advantage; the second is fortuitous, the third is almost incredible. The first three do not make a case *per se* for intervention since it has to be asked why market forces—principally the landlords—do not respond without it. The fourth supposes not only a social judgement that one can get value for money this way, but also that ways can be found of syphoning off the benefit so that it does accrue to the landlord or to new richer tenants rather than to the poorer old tenants. But redistribution through subsidy aside, the case for intervention on the grounds of improving efficiency must be the Prisoners' Dilemma. It will not surprise the reader to learn that an economist sees blight as a social cost which one property may impose on another and which may be a reciprocal relationship. To simplify, let us assume that one owner considers whether to decorate and improve his property, believing that he can gain a higher rent from the flats into which it is divided. If his neighbours whose properties are also divided into flats were to follow, they would be able to charge higher rents, each one of them, than if only the first landlord improves his property. In the absence of collusion, it must pay landlords not to improve their property. If their neighbour does so, there is a possibility that by raising the tone of the neighbourhood they will be able to charge higher rents for zero outlay. They cannot be worse off. The interesting possibility is where it is not profitable for one or a handful of landlords to improve their property, but where if all in the neighbourhood were to do so simultaneously the increased rents would justify the capital expenditure. It is this that is the justification for urban renewal on efficiency grounds. There is a built-in incentive against any one owner beginning the process of up-grading, and therefore areas may remain blighted indefinitely. In certain extreme cases it is one of the most plausible explanations of quite large-scale abandonments of poor quality housing in major American cities. When a few houses in a block become inhabited by criminals, drug addicts and tramps, their presence can pull down the rent that other landlords can charge to such an extent that it is more profitable to abandon the building than either to rent or to sell it.

If blight is left to market forces, what one would expect over time is some improvement at the fringes of blighted areas where they are adjacent to areas of better-quality housing. Here it may be easier for landlords or new purchasers to improve such houses so that they come to be seen as part of the better area rather than of the worse. Some might argue that if an area has the potential for profitable rehabilitation or redevelopment if this is done simultaneously, it should be profitable for a larger developer to acquire the properties and develop them collectively. In principle this could be so, but the private developer faces certain difficulties. The costs of acquisition may be high. The more properties he acquires, the clearer his intentions will become. The properties remaining outside his ownership, but which he needs to complete his site for redevelopment, will rise in price to him as their owners see their bargaining power. Since some part of the profit from redevelopment accrues to some landowners in this way, and not to the developer, there will be less redevelopment. In practice many areas will not be redeveloped at all. In these circumstances, local authorities, using their powers of compulsory purchase, may achieve what the market cannot. They can buy all the property at its value given its existing use, redevelop it as a parcel and therefore realize the capital gain. It is important to stress that it is an implication of the Davies and Whinston approach, and necessary if urban renewal is to be regarded as efficient from the market standpoint, that urban renewal does realize a profit through appreciation in site values. In general terms this means that the result of such urban renewal will be the replacement of lower-valued by higher-valued uses. Therefore if the argument put forward for planned development is that it can realize potential value which unplanned development cannot, it follows that a local authority which buys up land and buildings should find the transaction profitable. If such a development is not profitable, it prompts the question whether the local authority is deliberately foregoing the profitability by over-compensating those whose property is expropriated, or by selling or renting the redeveloped property at less than market value. The implication is that if it is doing either of these, it is embarking on a policy of subsidization to achieve some redistributive end. If one looks at the matter in this way, one is encouraged to ask what would have been the most profitable use of the land and therefore how much real value has been foregone by adapting it to some less profitable use. One is here making an important distinction between a planner intervening where the market fails to achieve an efficient solution and achieving that solution; and a planner intervening to achieve a different solution.

Before considering intervention to achieve non-market solutions in more detail, it is useful to consider a few of the traditional planning problems, and also some criticism of the planner's need to intervene.

1. *Highway planning* is an example of a public service or investment which it is scarcely feasible to imagine private enterprise providing, if for no other reason than because of the monopoly power private ownership would confer.

2. *Pedestrian and vehicular segregation* brings in at least two kinds of divergence between private and social cost. (*a*) Vehicles and people getting in each other's way do impose congestion costs on each other which ordinary market forces cannot deal with. (*b*) Segregation reduces accidents. The market does not work so as to produce an efficient solution here either.

3. *Zoning* can be justified by the Prisoners' Dilemma argument. By requiring everyone in an area to achieve and maintain certain standards, it establishes the 'tone of the neighbourhood' and raises average property values and rents.

4. So too can a large number of *building and planning* controls be justified. For example, it may be in no one landlord's interest to achieve social optimal levels of construction and maintenance so as to make his house healthy, if his neighbours do not follow his example. However healthy his house, he or his tenants are at risk to infectious and contagious disease starting elsewhere. The same is true of fire regulations. If such regulations are truly efficient, they will raise property values and rents to reflect reduced risks (and insurance coverage).

5. The same argument applies to the construction of *new towns*. The principles here are that there are benefits of the Prisoners' Dilemma type to be realized from the simultaneous planning and controlled development of a new town. If the principles guiding the construction of a new town were

those of economic efficiency, there should be a profit to the developer measured by the difference between the land values in their previous use and land values after development. A new town will also achieve external economies of scale in the labour market and the inter-relationship between the firms located there, which should mean more efficient production and hence a reduction in costs. Because the original landowners, particularly those who wait to sell last, may hold the developers up to ransom, there are advantages in such a development being done by public enterprise, though this is probably less compelling where there is a reasonably free land market than for redevelopment within a city.[1]

To find theoretical justification for planners intervening in the market because of inadequate information, what we have called market failure, is one thing. To argue that actual interventions by planners improve on the performance of the market is another.

One argument we have already met with is that admitted divergences between private and social cost, from the standpoint of the individual, can be dealt with by the large developer, as in the case of urban renewal or a new town, almost as well as by the state. A more thorough-going argument on these lines

---

[1] There are strong but different reasons for thinking a private-enterprise new town improbable in most parts of Britain. To be profitable there must be significant differences between ex-ante and ex-post land values. In the United States, new town developers acquire land considerably beyond the fringes of the built-up area for which it is to be a satellite. In doing this they reduce land acquisition costs, firstly because land costs are initially lower, but secondly because there is so much land on which they could build that the existing landowner has little bargaining power to up the price. In Britain it is almost impossible that a developer could find a sufficient area of land with planning permission for housing. If he could, much of the increase in land values would already have accrued to the landowner and not the developer. If he had to co-operate with a landowner in order to get a change of use permitted by the planning authorities, a sizeable proportion of the appreciation in values would once more accrue to the landowner. The situation is a consequence, first, of the relative scarcity of land in the more urbanized parts of Britain, but more importantly, of a system of land-use controls which, in cases like these, works to the advantage of the landowner.

F

by Siegan maintains that private enterprise working through legal agreements can produce superior solutions to those achieved through zoning ordinance in the United States.[1]

The contrast Siegan makes is between a number of Texas cities, particularly Houston, where there are no zoning ordinances, and other U.S. cities where there are. A few planning controls exist in these Texas cities. There are minimum plotsizes in Houston; it is not clear whether the justification for this would be that advanced earlier in this chapter. There are also ordinances requiring new houses to have a certain number of garages related to the number of bedrooms (which might be justified rather dubiously in terms of reducing congestion on the streets by the removal of parked vehicles). Some other cities have ordinances restricting mobile homes and signboards.

These cities do not have the typical North American zoning ordinances which specify building and land-use within subdivisions: for instance, to ensure that a subdivision is built of single-family homes of similar value. Siegan's proposition is that the same effect is achieved more efficiently by legal agreements between private parties. He argues first that the normal workings of the market help to achieve separation of land uses. One does not get heavy industry in residential sections (i) because land costs tend to be high, (ii) because the prime requirement for such industry is access to motorways; and (iii) because industry would anticipate a heavy cost in having to acquire staff to deal with a constant volume of written and telephone complaints over noise, smell and heavy traffic, as well as the effects on the neighbourhood of early and late working hours. Similarly, market forces keep most shopping and commercial developments off ordinary streets, since all private interests concerned know that the most profitable sites for these are near expressways and major traffic interactions. Mixed uses are much more likely to be encouraged by market forces in lower income areas.

If the market achieved what everyone wanted, there would be no need for legal covenants. Virtually all developers of sub-

---

[1] B. H. Siegan, 'The Houston Solution: The case for Removing Public Land-Use Controls', *Land-Use Controls Quarterly*, Vol. 4, No. 3, Summer, 1970.

divisions use such agreements to limit the use of homes to single-family occupation. In the wealthier areas, as Siegan points out, these agreements manage to secure what zoning ordinances in other cities are not legally able to do. There they have 'virtually forbidden any construction that might injure values' and have established certain 'architectural and aesthetic standards'. There are also similar legal agreements on some industrial estates. Agreements concluded since World War II contain 'automatic extensions provisions'. They continue after the first period, usually twenty-five to thirty years, for successive periods of ten years unless at least fifty-one per cent of owners agree to amend them.

Siegan recognizes that one reason why such agreements, even if undertaken, are less likely to be enforced in the lower income quarters is the cost of enforcement. This, however, is mitigated because, by an ordinance, the city has taken on itself the duty of enforcing such agreements. Siegan argues that they are still less likely to be enforced because (i) lower income families are less interested in single-family occupation as such, (ii) because they are more likely to value the chance of capital appreciation if they should be able to sell their property for redevelopment and (iii) because their tastes are lower than those of the wealthy.

There are four separate issues to be discussed here:

1. Siegan's interest would seem to be purely in the Prisoners' Dilemma kind of situation. The higher the land values within a subdivision, the clearer the indication that the land is being used most efficiently and that the interests of the owners and tenants are being served. The notion that one would impose restrictions on people which they did not recognize to be in their own interest, is quite foreign to the analysis. Among landowners, the only losers are any renegades who, for example, would like to subdivide their homes and take in lodgers rather than move. The justification for preventing them doing this is that the values of other people's houses taken collectively would fall by more than the renegade would gain.

2. Zoning and legal agreements become two ways of correcting for market failure. They are essentially alternative administrative arrangements. What is lacking is any examination

of their respective merits as such. One would like to know the administrative costs of the two methods. Relying on litigation could be expensive. The implication would seem to be that any comparisons here are dwarfed by other factors. As Delafons has pointed out, there is a substantial suspicion of controls operated through local government because of the opportunities this gives for graft.[1] A strong argument for a legal agreement approach is that it does not give such opportunities, at least so far as the wealthier citizens are concerned. A reason Siegan does not discuss which could explain why the political authorities do not enforce such legal agreements in poorer areas, could be that the poor do not carry the political weight to make enforcement worthwhile. Whether the opportunities for corruption and undue influence in the granting of planning applications in Britain are sufficient to make it worth considering the alternative of legal agreements is an interesting question. Britain is usually judged to be far less corrupt than the United States. Moreover it is doubtful, as we have seen, if less rich citizens would gain from the chance, though in British cities it is arguable they would not lose.

3. Houston is a much younger city than most British cities, and the legal agreements only apply effectively to subdivision built over the last twenty-five years. While a developer can act as the intermediary who draws up a legal agreement for prospective purchasers, who could do this for an existing area? Even if the planner or some other official were to do this, or if some owners were to hire a lawyer to persuade other owners for them, it seems improbable that one could get a sufficient proportion of owners to sign to make the operation worthwhile. If it were to be given political force, so that, for example, such an agreement were to be enforceable if some stated majority of owners agreed, it would raise problems of compensating the minority which would not arise for a new development.

4. Even so, Siegan has a major point. He argues in effect that there are other reasons for supposing that zoning ordinances

---

[1] J. Delafons, *Land-Use Controls in the United States*, M.I.T., 1969, pp. 6, 7.

are less effective than legal agreements in protecting the interests of landowners. For example, in many American cities in recent years there has been a boom in the construction of high-rise suburban flats. Many cities have given way to this and have allowed these in areas previously zoned for single-family occupation in spite of the protests of those families, and with the implication that the values of their homes are as a result lower than they would otherwise be. In Houston, where would-be developers are unable to bring political pressure to bear to such a conclusion, there has been a much greater segregation of such developments in the areas which, for one reason or another, have been least resistant to them and which presumably put less value on keeping them out. Or, to take an example which is perhaps even more important for Britain, Houston has certain unrestricted strips where anything may be located. In general these are areas where no agreements obtain. In cities where planning controls cover virtually the whole area, all sorts of people are spending time to persuade the local authorities to change the zoning laws and let them in. In the United States the majority of such applications are successful. In Houston, because there are these 'free' zones, such people are far more likely to head for a site in these because it will be much cheaper for them administratively to do this than to persuade enough parties to a legal agreement. (Clearly this benefit could be achieved within a system of planning controls by designating enough 'free' areas.)

Siegan's point is that we have no way of knowing how far short zoned cities fall from the most efficient (profitable) use of land and buildings. The same is true of the operation of planning controls in Britain. One may assume that those who fix or amend zoning ordinances have in mind as a dominating consideration that they are there to serve the financial interests of those zoned. As we have argued earlier a number of regulations and restrictions will on average serve those financial interests. But excessive regulation will not. If one has an area whose houses are not attractive enough to rich enough people to afford the low densities at which they have been developed in single family occupation, there is a strong case for relaxing some or all the zoning requirements. The owners are worse off than they would otherwise be; and the land is being used with less than maximum efficiency. Similarly, in principle it is possible to justify public health and fire regulations as possibly increasing efficiency. There is some set of standards which will reduce the risk of disease and fire to the level which owners and tenants would find it in their best interests to afford. In so far as there are public costs of fire and disease, there may be a case for raising the standards further to reduce the incidence of consequential expenditure on the public authorities. In short, an evaluation of such standards could be undertaken to establish approximately what standards and regulations would be most efficient given all the interests concerned. But the danger of zoning and other planning control systems is that the standards will be misconceived, either too low or too high, or simply inept. Where planners, fire chiefs, public health inspectors and others with a professional bias operate systems of control, the danger is that controls will be excessive in that their costs in terms of lost efficiency will be great, even when all appreciable social costs and benefits are taken into account.

This is the case that any defender of zoning in the United States, or of planning controls, has to begin by answering. To adopt the method Houston approved is not a feasible alternative for areas already developed, even if it was thought desirable on other grounds. Neither, as we have seen, is there any reason to suppose that a bonfire of controls would produce the most efficient solution (though it is not impossible that it would produce a more efficient solution than the present one).

What is required, therefore, is an evaluation of planning controls to establish how far they match up to efficiency criteria. Short of these, there are outward and visible signs that other than efficiency criteria could be at work, even though one cannot prove that any particular instance is a sign of distortion. The most significant of these is that adjacent and similar land command very different prices. The most important determinant of the value of land is *accessibility*. This is a complex concept, meaning in general that a parcel of land tends to be highly valued if it is near other highly valued parcels of land which also mainly derive their value from accessibility. One consequence is that land near the centre of cities tends to be most highly valued, and that values diminish with distance from the centre. As an overlay on this pattern, land prices will tend to be greater nearer main roads and public transport stations. As an overlay at a finer level, corner properties in shopping areas tend to have higher values because of greater accessibility. As many observers have noted, this may mean considerable variations in the value of adjacent properties. Therefore the interpretation of price differences is a complex matter, but some kinds of difference do suggest the operation of non-market forces.

An example is the very great difference in land prices on either side of the boundary separating an urban built-up area from its green belt. If market forces were at work, one would expect the value of land at the edge of the city to be roughly equal to the value of agricultural land just beyond. If the value of the built-up land is very much higher, not only does this indicate that building would spread into the green belt if it were allowed, but it gives some guidance on the inefficiency of the situation. Land values on both sides of the green belt are higher than they would be without it, and this has many effects, including the encouragement of a higher residential density than would be efficient within the city, and in general a higher cost of housing with consequent effects on the demand and supply of housing. These are in some sense the 'price' the community is paying for the green belt. In general, through much of England, the very great difference between the cost of land for which permission to build houses has been given, and that for which it has not, is an indication of inefficiency. Quite apart from all the other subsidies to agriculture, it constitutes another subsidy, keeping the price of agricultural land in many areas low (while keeping the price of housing land high). Similarly, within cities a marked price difference between land which is or may be used for offices and that zoned for industrial or residential uses may also be a sign of inefficiency. The community may be sacrificing a not insubstantial amount of real income.

One comment planners and others may have on the argument so far is that it assumes the values of the market place. The discussion has been about market failure, and the implication is that it is the function of planners to do what they can to correct these market failures without introducing values of their own, or of the political process. While it is an over-simplification, one can say that if they were to act successfully to offset market failure, the operation of the land markets would be such as to achieve the pattern of land and building use which was most efficient in the sense that it would be reflected in the highest feasible gross national product. There may be other distortions and examples of market failure elsewhere which would mean that the nation was not achieving the most efficient use of its resources, but so far as land and building use was concerned, it would be making the most productive contribution to the national real income.

One can go somewhat further than this and introduce the notion of compensation. If one considers the smoky chimneys of a factory which is polluting some residential sections of a town, there is no question that the effects of the smoke pollution are externalities. There may, however, be a problem of deciding who should compensate whom, or on what basis negotiations should take place in order to reach an efficient outcome. A commonly adopted principle is that the first-comer should be compensated. If the houses are built around the factory, then the factory should be compensated if it is to change its methods of production in the interests of those who live in the homes. Conversely, if the factory was sited after the homes, the net cost of such an environmental change could be more reasonably required to be met by the factory. There are difficult marginal cases. Suppose the factory came first, but its method of production has changed since it arrived and after the houses were located, so that it now causes more pollution than it did. Or suppose that although the houses came first, the kind of people living in them, or their tastes, have changed. When the factory came it had no reason to suppose that those living around it minded the pollution, but perhaps some generations later, when pollution had become an issue, their successors did mind. To take a slightly different case, perhaps no one knew that a chemical was harmful when the factory began production, and it is only as a result of scientific progress that people have become aware of its damaging effects. Therefore in practice it may be difficult to decide who should be compensated and who should pay compensation, even if the assumption can be made that those who were there first should be compensated. As a principle it is analogous to *Caveat Emptor*. The presumption is that anyone who follows someone else into a neighbourhood should be able to appreciate the benefits and costs of being in that neighbourhood in making his location decision. If it is worth his while, either singly or in collaboration with others, to affect a change in that neighbourhood, then he must be prepared to pay for it. There is a famous nineteenth-century case given by R. H. Coase.[1] There was a pastry-cook in Wimpole Street who used two mortars and pestles for his business in a room at the back. One pestle had been working for six years, the other nearly thirty. A doctor moved in next door and was not worried by the machinery until eight years later he built an extension in his garden, back-to-back with the pastry cook's room in which the machinery was. The doctor wanted to use this extension as a consulting room, but found that the vibration and noise was such he could not use his stethoscope. He got an injunction from the courts to stop the pastry-cook using his machinery. The grounds were, in effect, that the doctor had reasonable expectation of being able to build an extension and use it without being disturbed by the machinery, however long it had been in operation. In this case, of course, and others like it, what is a reasonable basis for compensation depends on knowing what the law thinks are the reasonable expectations of those concerned. The relevance of this to planning is that many of the distributional questions that arise result from the belief that there is insufficient compensation. The poor are said to be severely affected by motorways because there tends to be a greater concentration of these towards the centre where they live. For various reasons, motorways in the centre of a town tend to be constructed in such a way that they cause a longer environmental shadow and have worse pollution and noise effects in the centre of a city than an equivalent mileage further out. Many would agree that those affected should receive more adequate compensation than the law tends to allow them now. The substitute principle might be to achieve what economists call a Pareto change: that is to make the effects of the construction of a motorway such that 'some are better off but no one is worse off'. This implies that compensation should be such that those affected are at least no worse off than they were before the motorway was built. While there

---

[1] R. H. Coase, 'The Problems of Social Cost', *Journal of Law and Economics*, vol. 3, 1960, pp. 1–44.

are severe measurement problems in ascertaining what the correct level of compensation would be and difficulties in planning questionnaires so as to avoid profitable falsehood, adoption of this principle would be a clear way of avoiding a great many distributional effects of planning and related decisions which are widely thought to be wrong. Alternatively, of course, it could be argued that everyone who occupies a dwelling ought to recognize that there is some expectation that his environment should deteriorate—that this is a known risk and to some extent reduces the compensation he should expect. In other words, the motorway is to be regarded like the 'doctor' in the Wimpole Street case. One has to plan on the assumption that it may arrive in the neighbourhood. Just what principles should govern compensation is not a decision for economists, but if a decision could be taken on these lines it would be easier to achieve efficient town-planning solutions avoiding a whole category of distributional consequences through paying the appropriate compensation.

A rather different argument would be that politicians and planners may wish to use planning to achieve redistributional ends. Thus, if it were possible, a green belt policy might be used positively to redistribute income from the richer to the poorer citizens. In fact it is not easy to see how this could be done systematically. A great many planning decisions do change relative land values. Thus to site parks, schools and other land-uses which are likely to increase land values in a neighbourhood which is poor, might seem to benefit the inhabitants relatively to those in rich neighbourhoods where perhaps fewer schools are built or parks established. In practice this may not benefit them more, particularly if, as is usual, most rent rather than own property. In that case the effects of such planning permission would tend to accrue to the landowner who may well not be poor, or even if poor, not especially among those the politicians and planners want to benefit. This problem arises constantly in the use of planning as a redistributive mechanism, simply because most planning decisions affect land values and so tend to affect the distribution of wealth and income as between property owners but only affects others indirectly. Moreover when the value of a property is improved, there is a tendency for it to be occupied by people or uses that can afford to pay more. There are, of course, ways in which it is possible for city governments to redistribute income between different groups in a city through physical planning, but these tend to be much more limited than one might think. However, even so far as this may be effective, it raises the question whether there are not normally more efficient ways of redistributing income.

Sometimes it is argued, as if it were sufficient contradiction of the economist's point of view, that other values rule than those of efficiency and conscious redistribution. If one looks at the lists of objectives and values which quite frequently preface urban plans, they embrace a wide variety of principles which do not at first sight reduce easily to efficiency or redistribution. But the economist is always asking that one should go beyond a general statement such as that it should be the concern of a plan to improve or protect the environment, to objectives formulated in terms of the individuals who will be affected by any such enhancement or protection. Is a measure one which they will pay for? If so, the planner may be doing no more than aiding or stimulating the operation of the market. Is it one that they would be prepared to pay for if there were no externalities and the market operated efficiently? Or is it that the planner would give more weight to environmental enhancement or protection than they would be prepared to pay for? If the last, one needs to ask—or so the economist would maintain— why is this redistribution to take place? Is it simply because one wants to make these people better off in a general sense so that in effect they have a higher real income per head? If this is the motive, there is usually much to be said for preferring straight transfers of cash which the recipients can spend as they please. Does one want to make them better off environmentally? If so, it begs the question whether they will recognize that they are in fact better off in an improved or protected environment. If environmental protection is the listing of interesting buildings, it is not improbable that a large number will feel no better off as a result. In many areas the same could be true if what was involved was a tidying up of streets and the painting of lamp posts. If one is concerned to improve or protect the environment, there would seem to be something to be said for trying to ascertain if the particular measures proposed are those that people would pay for if, say, their incomes were larger than they are, and if they were under any constraint to spend this money one way or another on improving their environment rather than on something else. Moreover, when a plan has a large number of such objectives, there would also seem to be something to be said for trying to ascertain how far the population affected would prefer that the money was spent on achieving one objective rather than another. We can generally assume that if redistribution takes the form of cash transfers then the recipients will be pleased, though those deprived to pay for the redistribution may well not be. The more one tends to specify the form the redistribution takes, the more probable it is the recipients feel they get less value than they would if it were a cash transfer. This leaves various ways in which the politician or the planner may be introducing what may loosely be called paternalism; a belief that he could override the values that affect people by his own. He may try to justify this. He could argue that many of the benefits of any plan will accrue to future generations, and that he thinks the values of future generations will be more like his own than that of their fathers or grandfathers. Or he may argue a different kind of paternalism—that he believes that, whatever people may think now, they will come to like the environment he provides for them so much that in retrospect they will admit they would have chosen as he chose before them. The difficulty, of course, is to provide any evidence that these justifications are likely to stand up. It is not impossible if, for example, it is a question of *per capita* income rising over time, that there may often in other cities be people as rich today as the next generation is expected to be in a presently poorer city. Similarly one may find relevant populations if the question is one of an expectation that industrial mix or system of tenure or some such similar structural variable will change. But all these possibilities raise a number of questions which one should perhaps bear in mind in any given case, though they may prove difficult to answer:

1. How far is it recognized that some planning and building controls serve genuinely paternalistic or redistributive ends rather than efficiency? Which do? Which do not, and to what extent?

2. Whatever these ends may be, do we have any idea of the extent of the efficiency or real income which is being sacrificed to achieve them? If we did, would we think all of this sacrifice worth it?

3. Even if we were to give as much weight to these ends when we had counted their cost, have we any reason to believe that the ways in which planning controls work are rational in relation to the ends they are meant to serve? If one aim of the system were to make it less profitable to be a landowner on the grounds that appreciation in land values is unearned increment, have we any reason to suppose that our system is less profitable for landowners? It is at least arguable that on average it is more profitable, and that within the average, the distribution of appreciating capital values between landowners is arbitary in many respects. If the poor were our concern, have we any reason to suppose that our system benefits them in any rational way?

4. Even if our system of controls were rational in relation to these ends, is there not a danger that the same ends could be achieved by other, non-planning, ends? For example, by income transfers in cash or kind between people, rather than through the mediation of a complex system of planning controls.

On arguments such as these rests the case for a thorough re-appraisal of planning controls—if not a bonfire, at least an intense bright light. Even if there is continuously to be disagreement over values, over the rôle of redistribution and paternalism, there may yet be much greater agreement that the efficiency of planning needs to be tested. I would expect that within the next ten years there will be increasing pressure to evaluate plans and planning controls, and that the outcome may well be revolution in planning methods and discipline. Increased concern for the environment may itself intensify the pressures of planners to be rational and to be concerned with efficiency. It is wrong to think that concern is mainly altruistic. People are becoming increasingly aware that their property values and their own standard of living depend greatly on pollution levels, congestion, whether their neighbours repaint their houses, crime in their neighbourhood and so on. Thus they have more incentive rather than less to press the city authorities to do things which are in their own interest and to avoid doing things which are in the interests of others, and the planner is likely to find more than ever before that he cannot ignore market forces.

Chapter Nine

Conclusions

EMRYS JONES

To a large extent the views expressed in this book are shared by all the members of the group who have contributed to it. Unanimity of opinion was not necessary but unanimity of concern was, and there was a very large measure of agreement about the way ahead and how the future problems of planning should be tackled. To the authors, therefore, the inter-relatedness of all the different aspects they were interested in was a basic assumption. The book obviously has been structured along specialist approaches, but nevertheless I hope that it has been clear to the reader that these are merely facets of one central problem and that there are many themes which recur time and time again. The purpose of this brief conclusion is to remind the reader of some of these main threads that have reappeared in various chapters and to bring us back to the central concern which underlay the whole notion of producing the book.

On the face of it the issues are simple. We are concerned in the first place with the quality of life and how to improve it; secondly, to what extent that achievement can be hastened and broadened to all segments of society by the part played by planning and planners; and thirdly, with a need for clarification of how issues will develop in the next thirty years and how they will be met by all the various aspects of planning—its techniques, its practitioners and the institution through which it works.

Quality of Life and Goal-setting

The quality of life in environmental terms is the departure point. In the past this term has been assessed in much too narrow a form. The environment means more than hedgerows, roads or bricks and mortar: it means more than pollution. Environment means a whole nexus in which life is lived. It must include people's expectations, their hopes and their aspirations. Consequently it involves judgement on the part of the planner of what people will want, and this is very closely bound up with the way in which the wealth of the country, which we assume will be increasing, is distributed. Peter Willmott envisages this as meaning that more people will share in the material advantages which are now the prerogative of the middle and upper classes. Planning will see its rôle in the future as less concerned with manipulating the environment, but rather as being involved in society as a whole and particularly with those segments which have qualities of life which are totally unacceptable. The answer to poverty is not in a planner's hands, but an appreciation of the total circumstances of the poor people—environmental and societal—is bound to become a necessity. A simple deterministic view about the curative powers of a recreated environment simply will not do. The planner must turn from the idea that the city is simply an artefact. Perhaps our concern with the city as a whole, and particularly with the regional implications of planning, has led to a danger of overlooking the small but highly emotive areas of disillusion and misery which are near the heart of so many of our cities. So far in Britain, such situations are still to a large extent objectively realized bits of the jig-saw which the planner and social ecologist fit into a background to give an academically satisfying picture of the whole. In the United States festering city sores have erupted, and students of the city have been forced to realize that they cannot dissociate themselves from the situation. A city—and its planning—must be seen through the eyes of the under-privileged, problem-oriented on a more intimate and much more personal scale. We have become beguiled by the products of our own analysis which have translated people into dots on plans, slums into neat areas of cross-hatching, misery into indices of shared facilities. Dry and abstract models, indices, eigen values, variables and principal components must all be translated back into flesh and blood. Recently the planner in this country has been urged to see and appreciate for himself the kinds of social ills for which he thinks he is prescribing. Involvement of this kind is a mere prelude to realization of the depth of the term 'quality of life', which comes easily to the lips of so many of us.

What we define as 'quality' cannot be dissociated from social values. David Donnison has argued elsewhere that the social scientist acts within a value system; a layman is entitled to know the ideology which lies behind the professional's actions, and the professional must be aware of the ideology of the community. Attitudes and aspirations must be clearly understood. 'The stance of the value-neutral social technologist will not do'. Indeed, Donnison goes further:

> Paradoxically it is only by recognizing that our work begins from and ends in social problems and evaluation that we can maintain its scientific rigour. Social scientists who claim that their conclusions are value-neutral and their prescriptions objectively valid, are often seeking to close debate by claiming sanctuary from criticism which might improve the empirical evidence and logical strength of their discipline if they were pressed home.[1]

The quality of life can only be understood, therefore, within specific value systems. This has long-term implications which may unfortunately seem irrelevant in the short run. In the latter case the present situation is changed only marginally and in a way unlikely to give rise to severe conflict. This is a step by step process which involves little risk, what Donnison terms a 'strategy of incrementalism'. In the long term, however, alternatives may be numerous. All their assumptions may have to be tested and validated by extensive data collection and analysis. It is much more speculative, yet it has to be within a firm and realistic framework and embody the value systems of those whose lives are being planned. Utopias are an easy way of by-passing these constraints, because they can lay down their own postulates. Paradoxically, too, increasing freedom to choose in the future means allowing for an unpredictability which may seem the very antithesis of planning. This kind of freedom of choice is one of the basic values we would want to respect.

The comprehensive and the incremental approaches are not by any means mutually exclusive. They can often be related to the scale of a problem, though it is by no means certain that they belong to either end of the same scale. Incremental

---

[1] Journal of Social Policy, Vol. 1, No. 2, April 1972.

decisions do not necessarily add up to a long-range goal; and long-range goals are hardly worth discussing in terms of alternatives if they are nothing more than a sum total of fortuitous or incremental changes. The formulation of goals is an essential prerequisite of initiating a pattern of incremental changes. The quality of life can only be tested against deep and far-reaching goals which concern society itself and the way in which it wants to live rather than with the details of the physical environment.

Complexities

The issues are exceedingly complex; the simple approach of the past is no longer possible. It is quite clear that as a series of systems, the city itself is incredibly complicated. Playing around with land-uses and manipulating the environment, with some implications perhaps of environmental determinants, is not enough. The planner can no longer even assume that what he thinks is the need of the community is in fact what the community wants. Derek Senior referred to the rather simple assumption about goals in the Abercrombie Plan. The issues which Abercrombie took for granted on behalf of society are now wide open. They have broadened beyond recognition. Planners in the old sense are ill-equipped to switch their activities from urban design to the problems of the proper application of national resources. For some time the planner has best operated as one of a team, calling upon a large number of specialists; and what is called for is not a simple solution, but a series of alternatives. Complex questions call for complex answers. This becomes perfectly clear in all the chapters. The setting up of social goals and the identification of a series of alternative ways of achieving those goals suggests that we are aiming at a rational manipulation of the processes involved. This also means that we are dissatisfied with the operation of the market as it is now. This does not necessarily mean that the operation of the market and the process of planning need always be in direct opposition. It is much too simple to say that more planning is an alternative to less market, as if these were the opposition of good and evil. Rather it will be the task of the planner in the future to identify those parts of the market operation which seem at variance with the goals of society and which do not fit in with the possible alternatives. But the chapter on planning and the market emphasizes how complex is the whole issue of information. Christopher Foster reminds us that a perfect decision is only possible when all the information is known. It is quite clear that most decisions, for example, are made very imperfectly. At the moment information is inadequate, unco-ordinated, available to a few only and often has to be bought. To some extent accessibility to information leads us back to the argument about inequalities and makes it clear that one of the first tasks in the future may well be equalizing opportunities or facilities for obtaining information, even though the information given to the public may be processed at a much generalized level. Already the need is obvious for large banks of data, but we have not sufficiently considered the problem of how the data are collected and who has access to them. It is quite reasonable to assume that collection of such data is a proper activity of planning departments of the local authorities. There must also clearly be a link-up between these data and regional and national banks. But access to the data might still prove to be a real problem, just as access to privately collected information would be jealously guarded by those who operate on a large scale within market forces; so there is a tendency for local authorities to regard their information as something that pertains to them but not to the public. Under the guise of professionalism on the one hand and a lack of comprehension on the other, there is a danger of a gulf widening between the planners and planned. This is something I shall refer to below. With reference to public participation, all we need to note now is that taxpayers have a right to see information gathered by their money and about their affairs. The complexity of their manipulation is something to be tackled and overcome.

Christopher Foster also reminds us of the need to clarify those issues where market forces can no longer cope. How far planning processes would be enlarged may well be largely a matter of how far market processes fall short of what is expected of them: again there are some areas of action which are on such a scale that they can only be undertaken by public authorities, for example the construction of public highways or the zoning of towns or even the building of new towns.

The final criterion by which market forces are judged is

efficiency. Rightly or wrongly, planning may well be judged in the same way. A plan works, or is good, if it is economically sound. Cost benefit analysis is made on this assumption and we have seen at least one major locational decision, that of the third London airport, couched in exactly these terms. The question arises as to whether planning must reach this criterion, at least before it is acceptable. By these criteria, in some aspects the market is operating acceptably and planning can very rarely increase efficiency measured on an economic base. However, this whole thing can be turned topsy-turvy by the application of social and economic criteria which lie outside the accepted premises. Again one can refer to the final decision of the third London airport which reversed the seemingly logical conclusions of the official inquiry.

However efficient the market force, it still leaves us with goals that lie outside the frame of reference of economic efficiency. To achieve these goals it is necessary to re-equip planners in the future, to see what rôle the government would have in operation, and what rôle the public will play, for instance.

The Future Planner

One thing that is certain about planners today and the agencies through which they plan, as well as the rôle played by the public, is our total inadequacy to meet the complexities of the future. The departmentalism of planning in practice today is a reflection of the fairly simply way in which planning issues were seen in the past. Departmentalism could be an enormous stricture upon planning in the future. As Brian McLoughlin suggests, what were once outputs in planning, and which possibly warranted vertical departmentalism, are now inputs; the real outputs concern policy and problem solving in relation to social goals. Above all, in meeting the new complexities of the situation the need is for new mixes of disciplines. It has already become quite clear in the last decade that planning is an inter-disciplinary activity and the so-called planner is one of a team. David Donnison reminds us that 'policy planning cannot be the preserve of any single profession'. In other words, he envisages that the priorities and strategies of planning should be determined by a unit which draws its data and its staff from

all departments which are vitally concerned. The most immediate task in the future is to recognize this and to formalize an
existing state of affairs. One way in which this could be done
would be to adjust the professional framework, allowing
membership of professional bodies to be open to all who are
concerned with planning issues although they have not
necessarily been trained specifically as planners.

The second necessary course is to see that the education of
the planner conforms to future demands. If we are looking
forward to a period when planning units and teams will be led
essentially by people concerned in urban management in a
wider sense, than this suggests that training must be set in
motion immediately to supply these new men. Peter Hall puts
forward a three-fold educational solution, that is, first a
generalist course as a preliminary which will not be confined
to the traditional aspects but rather will cut across the usual
boundaries of the social sciences. This would be followed by a
specialist technical course which would be mainly vocational.
Here all the complexities of the systems analyses, data banks
and so on, would be dealt with. The output would be a person
well equipped for junior management jobs. Beyond this again
there should be an advanced course of training on co-ordination
and strategic planning, and the people so trained will eventually
become urban managers. This, of course, makes nonsense of
professionalism as it is today. Rather it makes for a further
generalization in education at both the first and the third
stages. To some extent the second stage is being tentatively met
by the several masters degrees which are now being taught in
some universities, though it is interesting to add that many of
these elaborate courses are the outcome of an intellectual
approach to the problem rather than a response to the needs
of practising planners. This does remind us that the gulf
between the education of planners and the practice of planning
is still a fairly considerable one and cannot be bridged without
better knowledge and more research.

The Administrative Framework

To some extent the new courses referred to above were meant
to meet the needs of planning at a regional level, and we are
reminded by David Donnison that the whole exercise of plan-

ning operates within a system of government which is largely hierarchical. But whereas there are many aspects of planning which are moving up from the strictly local, through the county level, to the regional—and this is bound to receive an impetus in the future—we are also reminded that others are moving down. The enlargement of scale and the subsequent inevitable centralization of decision is seen as a danger. The public must be involved at a much more intimate level. The plea here is for neighbourhood council, community forums, action groups and other groups of this kind which have been suggested. Decision-making must take into account ideas and aspirations at this level. The great question is whether the future will see a formalizing of this neighbourhood level. In one way this refers us back to a problem which arose at the very beginning, and that is the need for a redistribution which refers not only to wealth and information but also to involvement. David Donnison certainly sees enormous strength in the future in these local councils, which would be augmented by professional groups and would in fact be a combination of professional social services, accountable leadership and community action.

Public Involvement

The local council on a neighbourhood level of involvement brings us to another recurring theme, that is the necessity for a much firmer link between the planner and the planned. At the moment it seems that the planned are involved only at what I have referred to as the incremental end of planning, where local decisions may impinge on personal liberties or where property rights are infringed, or amenities threatened. Derek Senior reminds us that there is a continuing need of machinery where such objections can be discussed: but the public inquiry in its present form—seemingly no more than an amalgam of such detailed considerations—seems so concerned with trees as not to be able to see the woods.

There is everything to be said for the idea that the public should be involved at a much more fundamental and earlier stage of planning—in fact at the structure plan stage and even at the setting of goals and the consideration of alternatives in the future: both the South Hampshire study and the Milton Keynes report made steps in this direction. Many planners would react to such an idea with dismay; increasing participation is seen as a further delay in an already long drawn-out process. The gap between planner and planned has been seen as greater than it is because participation has been transformed into confrontation at a stage when plans are near finality and planners feel themselves committed. As a result these exercises are often an exercise in public relations—though even as such they are often disastrous.

Milton Keynes provides a good example of what can be done, however fumblingly. It was a step in the right direction. An interim report was published in February 1969 which was not 'a definite plan for building the city . . .' but 'enabled the ideas which will be developed for the new city to be discussed and considered at an early stage by the public and by organizations and authorities concerned'. To meet this obligation to the public, twenty-five meetings were held in and near the designated area, which then had a population of about 45 000, and the Press gave a supplementary covering. The meetings were combined with exhibitions and questionnaires were available for people to make their comments. Eighteen thousand notices were distributed, together with an outline of the proposals and a copy of the questionnaire. It is calculated that twelve per cent of the adult resident population attended the meetings. They were 'immensely valuable to the planner in identifying the main issues with which the public was concerned'. Four hundred and fifty questionnaires were returned which showed that a small minority were very deeply involved.

The final report of Milton Keynes was prepared against the background of this public participation, but in addition to helping the planner in identifying feelings about certain issues, it has served a very valuable purpose in explaining exactly what the planners had in mind.

The aim should be to explore the values of society, to gauge the changing values and to express these within the social goals and their implementation. Perhaps this will overcome, to some extent, the difficulties of professionalism with which planning is beset today. It does not preclude the necessity of the planner making strategic or alternative proposals quite explicit. In the Milton Keynes proposal it is stated, 'the more technical the problem—the more imperative it becomes that the nature and implication of proposed populations be presented comprehensively and lucidly in long terms, both for informing the public of the overall effects of these solutions, and to obtain comments and opinion on them.[1] Openendedness, flexibility, the indeterminate element in planning which can best accommodate change—these do not preclude the need for discussion at all stages. Indeed they demand more rigorous approach and a more enlightened public, as well as a more enlightened planner.

The future, therefore, calls for these things: first, a greater concern with the quality of life; second, an appreciation of the complexity of the problems involved, and of the techniques by which these problems can be solved; third, a new kind of planner, broader in his outlook and conviction than ever before; fourth, at every scale in the hierarchy of administration, as much involvement as possible of the public; fifth, participation of the public in planning which will lead to identification of the goals for which planner and planned are aiming, although this may mean new techniques of participation which have yet to be explored.

---

[1] *The Plan for Milton Keynes*, Vol. II, 1970, p. 110.

Index